AMERICALISM

Rebuilding the American Dream Together

No One Left Behind

ButterflyMan

Independent Thinker

NOT LEFT · NOT RIGHT · ONLY AMERICAN

Published by ButterflyMan Publishing LLC
United States of America

First Edition

For inquiries:
contact@butterflyman.com
www.butterflyman.com

ISBN: 979-8-90217-016-7

Foreword

Why Americalism

Most Americans do not truly understand what socialism or communism mean in theory.

They understand those words emotionally.

To most Americans, *socialism* and *communism* are not abstract economic models or policy frameworks. They are inseparable from images of the Soviet Union, Mao's China, political repression, shortages, and the loss of freedom. Whether those associations are historically complete or intellectually precise no longer matters. Emotionally and culturally, the language is already poisoned.

In the United States, even the *sound* of those labels triggers rejection.

That reality cannot be ignored.

One afternoon over lunch in Midtown Manhattan, I was talking with an old friend, Larry. I told him that I wanted to show Americans the *useful* and *human* elements often mislabeled as "socialist"—the dignity, security, and balance found in parts of Northern Europe. But I admitted the real obstacle was not the substance of the ideas. It was the name.

As long as those ideas carried the label *socialism*, most Americans would never listen.

Larry paused, thought for a moment, and then said simply, "Why don't you call it **New Americanism**?"

That moment mattered.

I had been struggling with language for a long time—not because the ideas were unclear, but because language carries history. Every familiar label came with baggage: ideological reflexes, political defenses, and inherited misunderstandings. What I needed was not a slogan, but a clean starting point.

I owe Larry credit for unlocking that problem.

In the end, I chose **Americalism**.

Not *New Americanism*, but *Americalism*—a name without inherited weight, without partisan residue, and without historical debt. A word meant to signal a new era rather than argue with the old one.

Americalism was born not as a correction of the past, but as a framework for what comes next.

It felt different.
It felt honest.
It felt open.
And most importantly, it felt American.

Northern Europe—especially in the coming AI era—offers a clearer picture of what a stable, humane future society can look like than either extreme capitalism or authoritarian systems. I explore this more fully in another book, *Utopia Humanity Society*. Countries such as Sweden, Denmark, Norway, and Germany did not succeed through ideology. They succeeded through balance: strong markets combined with dignity, fairness, and shared responsibility.

America itself once understood this.

Some of the strongest and most confident periods in American history occurred when taxes on extreme wealth were high, public investment was robust, and society was more cohesive. These were not eras of decline. They were eras of expansion, innovation, and national confidence.

For the past forty years, however, America has been trapped in a single belief: that tax reduction alone is the solution to every problem. The results are now clear. Government capacity has been hollowed out. Infrastructure has decayed. Public trust has weakened. We struggle merely to maintain what previous generations built—let alone improve upon it.

That experiment has run long enough.

It is time to change—not through ideology, not through imported labels, and not through division.

Americalism is not socialism.
It is not communism.
It is not extreme capitalism.

It is a distinctly American answer to a distinctly American crisis.

And it begins with a simple belief:

A society is strongest when dignity, democracy, and responsibility move forward together.

Contents

Preface

A Note to the Reader
Why this book exists
Why the old language no longer works
Why America needs a new civic vocabulary

PART I — THE BROKEN PROMISE

Chapter 1 — The American Dream, Unfulfilled

What America promised
What millions now experience
How dignity quietly disappeared

Chapter 2 — When Democracy Became an Auction

Money in politics
The rise of oligarch influence
Why voting alone is no longer enough

Chapter 3 — Inequality Without Shame

Extreme wealth concentration
The myth of "trickle down"
Why imbalance destabilizes societies

PART II — HOW AMERICA BROKE ITSELF

Chapter 4 — America Is Not Too Expensive — America Is Broken

Why higher wages no longer fix affordability
Loss of domestic capability

When a nation stops making things

Chapter 5 — Fast Capital, Low Quality Life

Disposable goods, disposable lives
Why everything costs more and lasts less
The hidden price of speed

Chapter 6 — The Global Illusion

Outsourcing as a temporary fix
Why the world can no longer subsidize America
The end of extraction economics

PART III — THE OLIGARCHY PROBLEM

Chapter 7 — When Wealth Merges with Power

What happens when billionaires buy politics
Lessons from history: Russia, China, Hong Kong
Why oligarchy always turns on its creators

Chapter 8 — Democracy Must Not Be for Sale

Campaign finance corruption
Super PACs and dark money
Restoring political equality

Chapter 9 — The Moral Failure of Extreme Wealth

Wealth without responsibility
Why taxation is not punishment
The American social contract revisited

PART IV — THE AMERICALIST ALTERNATIVE

Chapter 10 — What Is Americalism?

Beyond left and right
Freedom with responsibility
A uniquely American civic model

Chapter 11 — The Dignity Economy

Why dignity is the foundation of freedom
Healthcare, education, housing as stability
Human wellbeing as national strength

Chapter 12 — Made Local: Rebuilding Capability

Why domestic production matters
The 25% Made Local framework
Repairing skills, supply chains, and communities

PART V — REPAIRING THE SYSTEM

Chapter 13 — Progressive Taxation as Civic Responsibility

Why the ultra-rich must contribute more
Historical evidence from America's strongest era
Taxation as economic engineering

Chapter 14 — Inflation Is a Capability Problem

Why interest rates cannot fix everything
Supply, skills, and structural limits
Stabilizing prices through production

Chapter 15 — Climate, Speed, and Civilization

Why overproduction drives emissions
Slowing the system without sacrificing life
Environmental repair through restraint

PART VI — A FUTURE WORTH BUILDING

Chapter 16 — A New Declaration of Interdependence

From radical individualism to shared responsibility
Why societies rise together—or fall together

Chapter 17 — Protecting Wealth by Protecting Democracy

A warning to oligarchs
Why dignity and democracy safeguard families and legacy
Choosing principle over short-term power

Chapter 18 — The Choice Before Us

Managed decline or deliberate repair
What happens if America does nothing
What happens if it acts

Epilogue

The Human Horizon
Why the system must serve the human
Why America can still rise
Why dignity comes first

Appendices

Preface

A Note to the Reader

This book is not written for one party, one ideology, or one generation.
It is written for a country.

America does not suffer from a lack of intelligence, innovation, or wealth. It suffers from something more difficult to name: a quiet erosion of dignity, balance, and democratic confidence. Many Americans sense this erosion every day, even if they cannot easily describe it. Life feels harder. Trust feels thinner. The future feels less secure than the past.

Public debate tells us to choose sides—left or right, capitalist or socialist, globalist or nationalist. But those arguments increasingly feel detached from lived reality. They explain less and divide more.

This book begins from a different premise:

> The core crisis of America is not ideological.
> It is structural and moral.

> When people work full-time yet cannot live securely, something is broken.
> When extreme wealth converts directly into political power, something is broken.
> When a nation can no longer maintain the basic systems of daily life—housing, healthcare, infrastructure, trust—something deeper than policy failure is at work.

Americalism is not a replacement ideology. It is a **civic repair framework**—an effort to restore the conditions that once allowed freedom, innovation, and prosperity to coexist with dignity and democracy.

This book does not ask you to abandon capitalism or embrace socialism. It asks a more fundamental question:

What is an economy for?
What is a democracy meant to protect?
And what responsibilities accompany success in a free society?

The answers are not radical. They are American.
Introduction

A Nation at the Crossroads

Some periods of history move slowly.
Others accelerate without warning.

We are living in the latter.

What the United States faces today is not a temporary economic downturn, not a single election, and not a passing political crisis. It is a deeper, structural challenge:

A system that was meant to serve the people is steadily drifting away from them.

This book does not ask the reader to choose a side.
Because the real problem has never been left versus right.

The real question is whether the system still revolves around human beings.

I. When Growth No Longer Means Progress

For decades, America relied on a simple equation:

Growth equals progress.
Wealth equals success.
Markets equal freedom.

That equation no longer holds.

Today:

- The economy grows, yet the cost of living rises faster.
- Wealth accumulates, yet concentrates in fewer hands.
- Technology advances, yet anxiety, illness, and social fragmentation deepen.

People work longer hours with less security.
They consume more yet feel less stable.
Institutions appear powerful, yet trust in them erodes.

This is not a failure of individuals.
It is a failure of structure.

II. When Money Replaces the Citizen

Democracy rarely collapses in dramatic fashion.
More often, it erodes quietly.

When elections depend on massive funding,
when legislation is shaped by lobbying networks,
when public policy increasingly reflects financial power
rather than public interest,

democracy shifts—from a system governed by citizens to a process influenced by money.

This is not conspiracy.
It is institutional drift.

As wealth and power merge, the voice of the citizen weakens, and social trust begins to dissolve.

III. America's Problem Is Not Ideology, but Direction

This book does not attempt to revive an old doctrine, nor to invent a new ideological label.

America does not lack ideas. It lacks direction.

It needs neither extreme market worship nor extreme state control.

It needs an answer to a more fundamental question:

> How can a modern society sustain long-term balance between freedom, efficiency, dignity, and stability?

IV. Americalism: A Civic Framework, Not a Political Movement

Americalism is not a political party.
It is not a movement.
It is not a belief system demanding allegiance.

It is a **civic framework**.

It seeks to reexamine three questions that modern systems have largely avoided:

1. **What is the purpose of a system?**
To serve capital—or to serve people?

2. **How should economic success be measured?**
By aggregate wealth—or by social stability and quality of life?

3. **What does freedom truly mean?**
The absence of constraint—or the presence of dignity and responsibility?

V. "No Left. No Right. Only American."

In an age of polarization, the most overlooked group is the ordinary citizen.

Children, workers, the elderly, the disabled, farmers, the unemployed, the homeless—
they do not live inside ideological debates.
They live inside daily reality.

Americalism does not ask where you stand politically. It asks whether the system still works for you.

That is why this book returns repeatedly to a single principle:

No Left. No Right. Only American.

VI. What This Book Will Examine

The chapters that follow will explore:

- Why outsourcing and globalization served as temporary fixes, not lasting solutions
- How the merger of wealth and political power weakens democratic foundations
- Why extreme wealth represents a moral and institutional failure, not merely inequality
- Why dignity is a prerequisite for freedom, not a byproduct of it
- Why manufacturing, agriculture, and local capability must be rebuilt
- Why progressive taxation is civic responsibility, not punishment
- Why inflation is fundamentally a problem of capability, not money
- Why climate stability requires structural balance, not austerity
- Why no one should be left behind

VII. The Author's Position

This book does not ask the reader to accept the author's authority.
It asks the reader to think.

It is not a call to mobilize.
It is a call to take responsibility.

If the United States wishes to remain a stable, free, and credible society, then its systems must once again be designed around people.

Closing of the Introduction

Civilizations do not endure by accident.
They endure by choice.

The choice to design systems that serve humanity—
rather than force humanity to serve systems.

This book is about that choice.

PART I — THE BROKEN PROMISE

Chapter 1 The American Dream, Unfulfilled

The American Dream was never about becoming rich.

It was about becoming secure.

For generations, the promise was simple and powerful: if you worked honestly, played by the rules, and contributed to your community, you could expect a stable life. You might not be wealthy, but you would not be disposable. You would have a place to live, healthcare when you were sick, education for your children, and the dignity of being needed.

That promise shaped the identity of the United States more than any slogan or constitution. It built trust between citizens and institutions. It created patience during hardship and optimism during change.

Today, that promise is breaking.

Millions of Americans work longer hours yet feel poorer. Housing costs rise faster than wages. Healthcare is treated as a financial risk instead of a social necessity. Education increasingly delivers debt before opportunity. Infrastructure decays while costs multiply. Even basic repairs—of homes, roads, appliances—have become expensive, delayed, and unreliable.

This is not simply inflation.
It is not simply globalization.

It is not simply technology.

It is the result of a system that gradually stopped serving people and began serving extraction.

When Prosperity Detached from People

Over the past four decades, American economic success became increasingly disconnected from American lives. Growth continued on paper, but stability eroded on the ground. Wealth concentrated upward while risk flowed downward.

This did not happen by accident.

Manufacturing moved offshore without replacement ecosystems at home. Financial markets expanded faster than productive capacity. Corporate incentives rewarded short-term returns over long-term resilience. Political systems adapted to money rather than citizens.

The result was a quiet transformation:
America remained rich, but Americans became insecure.

The dream did not collapse overnight. It thinned. It frayed. It became conditional—available to some, denied to many, inherited by a few.

Dignity as the Missing Measure

What disappeared first was not income, but dignity.

Dignity is the feeling that your life is not fragile, that one illness or job loss will not erase you. It is the confidence that society recognizes your contribution and protects your basic humanity.

An economy can grow while dignity collapses.
A democracy can function while legitimacy erodes.

That is the danger America now faces.

The American Dream was never a guarantee of wealth. It
was a guarantee of **standing**—a place in society that could
not be easily stripped away. When that guarantee weakens,
resentment grows, trust dissolves, and politics becomes
vulnerable to manipulation.

People do not turn against democracy because they hate
freedom.
They turn against it because it stops protecting them.

The Quiet Redefinition of Success

At the same time dignity declined, success was redefined.

Success became speed.
Scale.
Market dominance.
Financial extraction.

Responsibility faded from the definition.

Wealth that once implied stewardship became detached
from obligation. Economic winners were no longer
expected to help maintain the system that enabled them.
Political influence became something to purchase rather
than something to earn through trust.

This shift laid the groundwork for oligarchy—not in name,
but in effect.

And history is unambiguous on this point:

when wealth and power merge, democracy becomes performative.

Why This Matters Now

This book is not nostalgic. It does not call for a return to the past. It recognizes that America has changed—and that the world has changed with it.

But it insists on one non-negotiable principle:

A free society cannot survive if dignity is optional.

The chapters that follow will examine how America reached this point, why conventional solutions no longer work, and what a dignity-centered alternative looks like—one grounded in American history, economic reality, and democratic responsibility.

Americalism begins here:
with the recognition that the American Dream is not dead, but unfinished.

And that finishing it is the work of our time.

Chapter 2 When Democracy Became an Auction

Democracy rarely collapses overnight.

It does not usually end with tanks rolling into parliament, nor with explosions that announce its death.

More often, democracy decays quietly—
while procedures remain,
elections continue,
laws are still cited,
and institutions keep functioning.

The danger begins when **decision-making power quietly shifts**,
while the appearance of democracy stays intact.

When democracy bends toward money, it does not immediately die.
It slowly loses its soul.

From Civic Politics to Money Politics

From its founding, the United States held a deep and instinctive fear of money ruling politics.

The architects of the republic understood something fundamental:
if wealth could be directly converted into political power, the republic would inevitably devolve into oligarchy.

For this reason, American democracy was built on a core principle:

Political authority should come from citizens, not property.

Yet over the past several decades, this principle has been steadily eroded.

Campaign costs have exploded.
Political parties have grown dependent on large donors.
Public service has quietly transformed into a capital-intensive industry.

A dangerous reality has emerged:

Not all voices carry the same weight.

When Elections Become Investments

In today's United States, a national election often costs hundreds of millions—sometimes billions—of dollars.

Where does that money come from?

Not from ordinary citizens,
but from a very small number of extremely wealthy individuals, corporations, and interest networks.

Under this structure, elections cease to be purely democratic expressions.
They become **investment mechanisms**.

- Money buys access
- Access buys influence

- Influence shapes policy priorities

These exchanges are not always explicit or illegal.
They occur through **legal, institutionalized channels**.

The result is a reality many recognize but few openly
acknowledge:

> **Some individuals possess more political
> influence
> than millions of citizens combined.**

Super PACs and Dark Money

The rise of Super Political Action Committees marked a
turning point in American democracy.

Formally, these entities are independent of candidates.
In practice, they can raise and spend unlimited funds to
shape narratives, influence elections, and dominate public
discourse.

Even more dangerous is the spread of so-called "dark
money"—
funds whose sources are hidden,
whose accountability is absent,
yet whose impact on public policy is immense.

This structure produces three corrosive effects:

1. **Collapse of transparency**
Citizens no longer know who is shaping
policy.
2. **Failure of accountability**
Power operates without public
responsibility.

3. Erosion of trust

Democracy begins to feel like a backstage
game.

When politics becomes incomprehensible,
citizens disengage.
When citizens disengage, democracy
becomes hollow.

From Representation to Agency

In theory, elected officials represent the will of the people.

In reality, many are forced to operate between two
competing roles:
- Representatives of citizens
- Agents of financial backers

This does not require moral corruption.
It is often the result of structural pressure.

**Without satisfying funding sources,
political survival becomes impossible.**

This is not primarily a failure of individual
ethics.
It is a failure of institutional design.

When political careers depend on wealth,
political judgment inevitably bends toward
wealth.

Oligarchy Is Not a Conspiracy—It Is a Trend

One point must be made clearly:

Oligarchy does not require conspiracy.

It does not need secret meetings or centralized coordination.

It emerges naturally when three conditions coexist:

> 1. Extreme concentration of wealth
> 2. Capital-intensive political systems
> 3. Weak or eroding regulation

> In such an environment, wealth gravitates toward power,
> and power reorganizes itself to protect wealth.

> History is unambiguous:
> when no firewall exists between economic success and political authority,
> democracy is hollowed out—legally, gradually, and quietly.

When Democracy No Longer Feels Real

The most dangerous shift is not institutional, but psychological.

When citizens begin to believe:

- Voting no longer matters
- Decisions are already made
- Politics serves only the powerful

Democracy loses its most vital foundation:
public belief.

Once belief erodes, society polarizes into two destructive responses:

- Withdrawal and apathy
- Anger and radicalization

Both weaken democracy itself.

Americalism's First Red Line

Americalism is unambiguous on this point:

> **Democracy must not be for sale.**
> **Politics must not be a commodity.**
> **Citizenship must not be priced by wealth.**

This requires:

- Ending unlimited political donations
- Restoring transparency and enforceable limits
- Rebuilding firewalls between wealth and power

This is not anti-capitalism.
It is **anti-oligarchy**.

It is not ideology.
It is a republic's instinct for self-preservation.

After the Auction Ends

When democracy is auctioned, the nation does not truly win.

In the short term, a few may profit.
In the long term, everyone pays.

Trust collapses.
Institutions hollow out.
Politics radicalizes.
Society fractures.

History offers no exception:

> **Oligarchy never produces stability—**
> **only deeper instability.**

The conclusion of this chapter is simple:

> **If democracy continues to be governed by**
> **money,**
> **America's problem will no longer be**
> **mismanagement—**
> **it will be regime decay.**

The next question is more uncomfortable still:

What happens when inequality loses all sense of shame?

Chapter 3   Inequality Without Shame

Inequality has existed in every society.

What distinguishes stable societies from unstable ones is not whether inequality exists, but **whether it is restrained, justified, and morally bounded**.

America once understood this distinction.

Today, it has largely forgotten it.

When Inequality Loses Its Apology

In earlier eras of American history, extreme wealth carried an implicit expectation of restraint.

Those who accumulated great fortunes were expected—socially, politically, and morally—to explain their success in terms of contribution. Philanthropy was not a branding exercise. It was a tacit acknowledgment that wealth, when too large, required justification.

That expectation has vanished.

Extreme wealth today is no longer accompanied by embarrassment, modesty, or even explanation. It is displayed openly, defended aggressively, and increasingly framed as proof of superior virtue or intelligence.

The language has shifted:

- From *"I was fortunate"* to *"I deserve everything I have."*
- From *"Success carries responsibility"* to *"Success owes nothing."*
- From *"The system helped me"* to *"The system is irrelevant."*

This is not merely a cultural change.
It is a structural and moral rupture.

The Myth of Merit Without Context

Modern inequality is often defended through a simplified narrative of merit.

Those at the top are said to be there because they are smarter, harder-working, more innovative. Those below are assumed to have failed—or not tried hard enough.

This narrative ignores reality.

No large fortune is created in isolation. Every accumulation of wealth depends on:

- Public infrastructure
- Legal systems
- Educated labor
- Political stability
- Enforced contracts
- Social trust

Markets do not exist independently of society. They are constructed, protected, and maintained by it.

To claim that extreme wealth is purely personal achievement is to erase the collective foundations that made it possible.

When wealth detaches itself from context, it also detaches itself from obligation.

From Inequality to Extraction

There is a crucial difference between inequality that emerges from productive contribution and inequality that arises from extraction.

Productive inequality reflects value creation.
Extractive inequality reflects value capture.

Over recent decades, a growing share of American wealth accumulation has shifted from the former to the latter.

This shift manifests in several ways:

- Financial gains disconnected from productive output
- Corporate profits driven by cost externalization rather than improvement
- Asset appreciation detached from real economic contribution
- Rent-seeking behavior protected by political influence

In such systems, wealth no longer signals usefulness. It signals **positional advantage**.

This is when inequality becomes corrosive.

The Psychological Toll of Visible Imbalance

Extreme inequality does not only affect balance sheets.
It reshapes social psychology.

When people see effort unrewarded and speculation rewarded, they internalize instability. When they observe rules applied differently depending on status, they lose faith in fairness.

This produces predictable outcomes:

- Declining trust in institutions
- Rising resentment across class lines
- Moral disengagement from civic responsibility
- Increased openness to demagogues

A society can tolerate inequality if it believes the system is fair.
It cannot tolerate inequality once it believes the system is rigged.

At that point, the question is no longer economic—it becomes existential.

When Wealth Rewrites the Moral Order

The most dangerous consequence of unchecked inequality is not poverty.
It is **moral inversion**.

When wealth reaches extreme concentrations, it begins to define norms:

- What is considered "reasonable"
- What is considered "earned"
- What is considered "acceptable"

Practices once seen as unethical become normalized. Behaviors once criticized are reframed as "efficient." Obligations are dismissed as interference.

In this environment, restraint appears naïve, and solidarity appears irrational.

The social contract frays—not because people reject it, but because they are taught it no longer applies equally.

Inequality and the Fragility of Democracy

Democracy depends on the assumption that citizens share a common fate.

Extreme inequality breaks this assumption.

When elites become insulated from public consequences—when their healthcare, education, housing, and security are detached from the systems used by everyone else—their incentives diverge.

They no longer experience public failure as personal risk.

At that point:
- Policy no longer reflects shared outcomes
- Political compromise loses meaning
- Governance shifts toward preservation of advantage

This is how democracies drift toward oligarchy
without formal constitutional change.

The law remains the same.
The experience of the law does not.

**Americalism's Second Principle: Wealth Must Carry
Responsibility**

Americalism does not oppose success.
It opposes **unaccountable success**.

Its position is simple:

> **When wealth exceeds any plausible
> relationship to individual contribution,
> it acquires civic responsibility.**

> This responsibility is not moral charity.
> It is structural necessity.

> Progressive taxation, wealth taxation, and
> political contribution limits are not punishments.
> They are mechanisms that prevent economic
> success from destabilizing democratic society.

> History is instructive here.

> The United States experienced its greatest
> period of shared prosperity when top marginal
> tax rates were high, investment was long-term,
> and capital was forced to reinvest rather than
> extract.

This was not a coincidence.
It was design.

The End of Shame Is the Beginning of Instability

A society in which inequality no longer feels the need to
justify itself is a society approaching rupture.

Not because people envy wealth,
but because they lose confidence that the system recognizes
human worth.

The issue is not that some have more.
It is that **too many are rendered invisible**.

The erosion of shame among the powerful is always
followed by the erosion of patience among the many.

History offers no counterexample.

Conclusion: A Choice Still Exists

America still has a choice.

It can continue to normalize extreme inequality and manage
the consequences—anger, polarization, instability.

Or it can restore boundaries, responsibility, and moral
proportion.

Americalism argues for the second path.

Not out of resentment.
Not out of ideology.

But out of a commitment to democratic survival.

The next question follows naturally:

What happens when economic speed destroys the quality of everyday life itself?

PART II — HOW AMERICA BROKE
ITSELF

Chapter 4   America Is Not Too Expensive

America Is Broken

Why Higher Wages, Lower Taxes, and Outsourcing Can No Longer Save the American Way of Life

For decades, Americans have been told a comforting explanation:

> The cost of living is rising because wages are too low.
> Raise wages, and affordability will return.

> This explanation feels reasonable.
> It is also **wrong**.

> Over the past decade, many Americans have seen their nominal incomes rise. In some sectors, wages have increased meaningfully. Yet life has become harder, not easier.

> Housing costs more but is built worse.
> Food costs more but tastes worse.
> Hotels cost more but feel cheaper.
> Appliances are cheaper up front but break faster.
> Repairs take longer and cost more.
> Infrastructure is patched repeatedly, yet fails sooner each time.

> This is not a paradox.

It is a diagnosis.

**America's problem is not insufficient income.
It is the loss of its ability to make life function.**

**When a Country Stops Making Things, Life Stops
Working**

There was a time when most of the essentials of daily
American life were produced domestically:

- Plumbing components
- Electrical systems
- Building materials
- Household appliances
- Tools
- Food inputs and processing

Alongside these goods existed something equally
important: **capability**.

People knew how to fix pipes.
Electricians understood systems end-to-end.
Parts were standardized and compatible.
Repairs were fast.
Infrastructure lasted decades.

When manufacturing disappeared, what vanished was
not only factories, but **entire ecosystems of skill,
standards, and experience**.

Today, America imports the objects of daily life but
has lost the networks that allow daily life to function
smoothly.

A leaking pipe can take weeks to fix.

Electrical work is expensive and inconsistent.
Appliances appear cheaper but cost far more over
their lifetimes.
Roads are resurfaced repeatedly yet deteriorate faster
each time.

Low quality is no longer cheap.
Low quality has become expensive.

Why Wage Increases Became Painkillers

In the past, raising wages improved living standards—
because the economy still possessed productive capacity.

Today, wage increases function more like painkillers: they
provide temporary relief while worsening the underlying
disease.

The reason is structural.

America no longer has flexible, competitive domestic
production. Essential sectors are dominated by a small
number of large firms. When wages rise, prices rise faster.

Rent increases.
Service fees increase.
Repair costs increase.
Insurance costs increase.

The additional income passes quickly through households
and flows directly into corporate margins.

The result is predictable:

- Higher wages

- Higher prices
- Worse affordability

People are not living better.
They are **paying more to stand still**.

Tax Cuts Did Not Create Growth — They Accelerated Extraction

Tax cuts have long been sold as fuel for innovation and investment. In a different economic structure, they might have been.

In today's America, tax cuts produced a different outcome: **accelerated extraction**.

Companies did not use tax savings to build factories.
They used them to buy back shares.
They did not invest in worker training.
They optimized pricing models.
They did not improve durability.
They reduced it.

Every dollar freed by tax cuts was pulled out faster, not reinvested deeper.

This made the economy look richer on paper while becoming structurally hollow—until inflation, fragility, and failure began to surface.

The World Can No Longer Subsidize America

For decades, America solved internal problems by exporting them.

Low-cost manufacturing from Asia.
Cheap consumer goods from Europe and Japan.
Energy and labor pressures absorbed elsewhere.

That model is finished.

Japan is aging.
Europe is strained.
Asia is no longer cheap.
Energy is constrained.
The planet itself is pushing back.

**There is no remaining external world from which
America can continue extracting stability.**

The old model did not merely fail.
It **ran out of world**.

Inflation Is Not a Monetary Problem — It Is a Capability Problem

Interest rates cannot create plumbers.
Wage hikes cannot manufacture spare parts.
Tax cuts cannot rebuild supply chains.

Today's inflation is the price of **missing capability**.

When a society cannot produce enough of what it needs
locally, prices drift upward permanently. Every shock
becomes inflation. Every delay becomes a cost increase.
Every repair becomes a luxury.

This is why inflation feels persistent.
Because it is **structural**, not cyclical.

The Radical Idea That Isn't Radical at All: Make Things Again

The solution is not to consume less.
It is to produce enough—locally, durably, competently.

This is the logic behind the **"25% Made Local in 10 Years"** framework.

Not 100 percent.
Not autarky.
Not nationalism.

Just enough domestic production to anchor prices, restore skills, and make daily life work again.

At roughly 25 percent local production:

- Prices stabilize
- Repair ecosystems return
- Quality improves
- Costs stop compounding

Life becomes predictable again.

Why High Progressive Taxes Are Not Punishment

In a fast, extractive economy, low taxes reward speed and short-term behavior.

High progressive income taxes do the opposite:

- They slow capital velocity
- Discourage short-term extraction
- Reward reinvestment

- Push money back into real production

Historically, America grew strongest when top marginal tax rates were high—not despite them, but because they forced capital to build instead of extract.

Taxation here is not redistribution.
It is **economic engineering**.

Climate Change: The Hidden Benefit of Slowing Down

The primary driver of emissions is not consumption itself, but **overproduction and rapid turnover**.

Fast cycles mean:

- More energy
- More shipping
- More waste
- More emissions

When products last longer and are made closer to home, emissions fall naturally—without micromanaging personal behavior.

A slower economy is not a poorer one.
It is a cleaner, calmer, more humane one.

What This Is Really About

This is not left versus right.
Not capitalism versus socialism.

It is about whether a society can still take care of itself.

Can it build?
Can it fix?
Can it maintain?
Can it live without constant stress?

A country that cannot maintain the basics of daily life
cannot remain stable—no matter how wealthy it appears on
paper.

Conclusion: Two Paths Forward

America faces two paths:

> 1.   Continue raising wages,
> cutting taxes, and managing
> decline—while costs rise,
> quality falls, and frustration
> deepens.

> 2.   Rebuild the foundations:
> production, skills, durability, and restraint.

> The first path is politically easier.
> The second is economically unavoidable.

This book argues for the second.
Not out of nostalgia,
but out of necessity.

Chapter 5   Fast Capital, Low-Quality Life

How Speed Became the Hidden Enemy of Modern Civilization

Modern America does not suffer from laziness.
It suffers from **speed**.

Over the past half-century, economic success has become
defined by how quickly capital can move, extract value,
and exit. Faster profits. Faster turnover. Faster growth.
Faster exits.

Speed is praised as efficiency.
In reality, speed has become **the primary driver of quality
collapse**.

When Capital Learns to Run Instead of Build

Capital once had to stay.

Factories required years to construct.
Workers needed decades to train.
Products were expected to last.
Reputation mattered.

Today, capital is mobile, abstract, and impatient.

It does not build ecosystems.

It arbitrages differences.
It does not repair.
It replaces.

Success is measured not by durability or contribution, but by **return velocity**.

The faster capital moves, the less responsibility it carries.

The Fast Everything Economy

America now lives inside a system of accelerated decay:

- **Fast food** that fills calories but damages health
- **Fast fashion** that lasts weeks and pollutes permanently
- **Fast housing** built cheaply and repaired endlessly
- **Fast hotels** that cost more but feel disposable
- **Fast appliances** designed for replacement, not repair
- **Fast logistics** stretching supply chains to fragility

Nothing is meant to endure.
Everything is meant to turn over.

Speed has replaced stewardship.

Why Quality Became "Inefficient"

In a fast-capital system, quality is a problem.

Quality takes time.
Quality requires skill.
Quality demands accountability.
Quality slows exits.

Durable goods reduce repeat sales.
Repairable systems reduce margins.
Local production reduces arbitrage opportunities.

So quality is redesigned out of the system—not because consumers asked for it, but because capital demanded speed.

Low quality is no longer a flaw.
It is a **business model**.

The Illusion of Cheapness

Americans are told they live in a world of abundance:

Cheaper goods.
More options.
More convenience.

What they experience is different.

Products cost less upfront but fail faster.
Repairs are expensive or impossible.
Replacement becomes mandatory.
Lifetime costs increase quietly.

What appears cheap is actually **extractive over time**.

The consumer saves today and pays forever.

Health, Stress, and the Cost of Speed

Speed does not only damage products.
It damages people.

Fast work schedules.
Fast service expectations.
Fast burnout cycles.
Fast psychological exhaustion.

When everything moves faster, nothing stabilizes.

Healthcare costs rise.
Mental health deteriorates.
Family life fractures.
Communities thin out.

A fast economy is not efficient.
It is **biologically incompatible** with human life.

Speed as an Energy Multiplier

Capital velocity correlates directly with energy
consumption.

Faster turnover requires:

- more shipping
- more logistics
- more packaging
- more production cycles
- more waste

Speed amplifies emissions not because people consume more, but because systems replace faster than they repair.

Climate change is not only about what we consume. It is about **how fast we cycle through the world**.

Why Markets Alone Cannot Fix This

In theory, markets reward quality.
In practice, markets reward **speed under concentration**.

When industries consolidate:

- price competition weakens
- durability becomes optional
- consumers lose alternatives

Choice becomes cosmetic.

Markets cannot self-correct when capital incentives reward exit over responsibility.

Slowing Capital Is Not Anti-Capitalism

This is not an argument against markets.

It is an argument against **unbounded velocity**.

Capital must move—but not faster than society can absorb.

Historically, America used:

- high marginal taxes

- reinvestment incentives
- antitrust enforcement
- local production requirements

These were not ideological constraints.
They were **stabilizers**.

They forced capital to stay long enough to build.

Quality Is a Public Good

Quality cannot survive if left entirely to short-term incentives.

Durability benefits everyone:

- lower lifetime costs
- stable prices
- lower emissions
- healthier lives
- resilient communities

But durability requires coordination.

That coordination is called **governance**.

The Americalist Correction

Americalism does not reject efficiency.
It redefines it.

Efficiency is not speed alone.
Efficiency is **life that works**.

The Americalist framework slows capital where it harms society and rewards it where it builds capability.

Key shifts:
- From turnover → durability
- From extraction → reinvestment
- From exit → responsibility
- From speed → stability

This is not nostalgia.
It is systems engineering.

The Civilizational Question

A civilization cannot outpace its own foundations indefinitely.

When speed exceeds skill,
when turnover exceeds trust,
when extraction exceeds repair,
collapse follows quietly.

Not in one dramatic moment,
but through daily inconvenience,
rising stress,
and declining dignity.

Conclusion: Relearning How to Stay

America does not need to slow down innovation.
It needs to slow down **extraction**.

It needs capital that stays long enough to care.

The next chapter examines how extreme wealth concentration—and the political power it buys—locks this fast-capital system in place.

Chapter 6 — The Global Illusion

Outsourcing as a Temporary Fix, the Transfer of Industrial Control, and the End of Extraction Economics

For decades, the United States believed it had solved a fundamental economic challenge.

If domestic production was expensive, move it abroad.
If wages rose, absorb the pressure through global supply chains.
If inflation appeared, import stability from elsewhere.

This logic appeared rational, open, and modern.
For a time, it even worked.

But it was built on a dangerous assumption:
that this arrangement was permanent.

It was not.

Outsourcing was never a long-term strategy.
It was a **temporary subsidy provided by the rest of the world**.

That subsidy is now ending.

Outsourcing as a Temporary Solution

Outsourcing did not begin as a mistake.

In the late twentieth century, global trade delivered real benefits:

- lower consumer prices
- rapid industrial scaling
- postwar reconstruction of allies
- deeper economic integration

For a period, outsourcing functioned as a mutually beneficial exchange.

The problem was not trade itself.
The problem was that outsourcing gradually became a **replacement**, not a complement.

Corporations stopped viewing overseas production as supplemental.
Governments stopped balancing openness with resilience.
Capital stopped reinvesting savings domestically and instead financialized them.

Trade turned into **extraction**.

What Was Lost Was Not Jobs, but Capability

The true cost of outsourcing was not employment alone.

It was **competence**.

Industrial ecosystems dissolved.
Skilled trades disappeared.
Supplier networks fragmented.
Repair cultures vanished.

America did not merely stop making things.
It stopped knowing **how** to make them.

At first, the global system concealed this loss:

- Asia provided scale
- Europe provided precision
- cheap energy and logistics filled the gaps

As long as the world remained cheap, stable, and cooperative, the illusion held.

But those conditions were never permanent.

From Follower to Competitor to Controller: China's Strategic Shift

Within the global outsourcing system, China was never a static participant.

It began as a follower.
Then became a competitor.
And eventually, in multiple critical sectors, evolved into a **structural controller**.

This transition was not accidental.

In its early phase, China entered global supply chains as the "world's factory":

- absorbing low-value manufacturing
- learning processes, standards, and technologies
- accepting thin margins in exchange for scale and experience

Superficially, this looked like passive integration. In reality, it was **systematic capability accumulation**.

Through long-term participation in outsourcing, China achieved three outcomes:

1. Internalized complete industrial chain architectures
2. Built deep engineering and manufacturing capacity
3. Learned how to operate—and strategically leverage—global rules over time

Outsourcing delivered more than orders. It delivered the **industrial operating system**.

Long-Term Control Versus Short-Term Competition

Unlike market-driven firms focused on quarterly returns, China did not optimize for short-term profit.

Instead, it pursued multi-decade strategies:

- targeted industrial subsidies
- sustained price suppression to displace competitors
- tolerance for long-term losses to gain market share
- upstream and midstream control over materials and components

This behavior appeared "inefficient" in the short term. In the long term, it proved structurally decisive.

Because this was not firm-level competition.
It was **state-level industrial engineering**.

When one system optimizes for speed and another for control, the outcome is not uncertain.

From Price Advantage to Irreplaceability

As Western economies continued outsourcing and dismantling domestic capacity, global control quietly shifted.

In key sectors such as:

- rare earths
- solar components
- batteries
- electronics assembly
- intermediate industrial inputs

China moved from participant to **gatekeeper**.

Global markets did not disappear.
But they became constrained by concentrated supply nodes.

Outsourcing changed in nature:
from a choice
to a dependency.

America's Strategic Miscalculation

America's miscalculation was not underestimating labor costs.

It was underestimating the power of **patient, coordinated, non-market industrial strategy**.

U.S. policy assumed:

- markets would self-correct
- price advantages were temporary
- technological leadership was non-transferable

These assumptions failed against systems willing to trade short-term inefficiency for long-term dominance.

When one side prioritizes quarterly returns and the other prioritizes structural control, leadership inevitably shifts.

Why the World Can No Longer Subsidize America

The global system that once absorbed American cost pressures has reached its limits.

- Asia is no longer cheap
- Europe is no longer stable
- logistics are no longer invisible
- energy is no longer abundant
- environmental limits are binding

The world can no longer underwrite American dependency.

The era of artificially low prices was not ended by policy.
It was **exhausted by reality**.

The End of Extraction Economics

Extraction economics relies on three assumptions:

1. Someone else absorbs the cost
2. Someone else bears the risk
3. Dependencies remain replaceable

All three assumptions are failing simultaneously.

When every nation seeks to extract, systems fragment:

- trade barriers rise
- supply chains are weaponized
- inflation becomes structural
- trust erodes

Globalization continues.
But **unaccountable extraction does not**.

Inflation as the Price of Dependency

Inflation did not arrive suddenly.

It surfaced when America could no longer import stability.

When supply chains fractured, energy costs rose, and logistics slowed, prices reset upward permanently.

This is not a monetary anomaly.
It is the **cost of lost capability**.

A nation that cannot produce enough of what it needs must accept the price set by others.

The Illusion Breaks

For years, the system appeared functional:

- shelves were stocked
- markets rose
- consumption continued

But appearances were sustained by external support.

That support is now withdrawing.

When external extraction ends, power dynamics shift inward.

Transition Point

Chapter 6 marks the end of the global illusion.

From this point forward, the book turns inward:
from external dependency
to internal power concentration

When global arbitrage ends, wealth seeks political protection.

That is how oligarchy begins.

Conclusion

America did not lose its position overnight.

It traded resilience for convenience,
capability for low prices,
and sovereignty for speed.

The world can no longer carry that burden.

What follows is not accidental.

When external extraction ends, internal control begins.

Chapter 7 — When Wealth Merges with Power

What Happens When Billionaires Buy Politics — and Why Oligarchy Always Turns on Its Creators

Oligarchy does not begin with evil intentions.
It begins with convenience.

When markets no longer provide easy profits,
when global extraction narrows,
when external subsidies disappear,
wealth turns inward.

It seeks protection.

This is the moment when money stops competing in markets
and starts **reshaping the state**.

The Merger That Ends Democracy

A healthy republic maintains distance between wealth and power.

When that distance collapses, the system changes in nature.

Politics becomes defensive.
Law becomes selective.
Democracy becomes procedural rather than substantive.

What emerges is not tyranny in the classical sense,
but **oligarchic governance**:
a system where a small concentration of wealth quietly
determines outcomes,
while democratic rituals continue.

Elections remain.
Institutions remain.
But real power migrates.

Why Wealth Always Seeks Political Control

Extreme wealth is inherently unstable without protection.

Large fortunes depend on:

- favorable tax structures
- regulatory exemptions
- monopoly tolerance
- legal asymmetries

Markets alone cannot guarantee these.

So wealth does what rational systems do:
it **buys insurance**.

That insurance is political influence.

At first, this influence appears limited:

- campaign donations
- lobbying access
- policy advisory roles

Over time, it becomes structural.

The Illusion of "Neutral Money"

Money is often described as neutral.
In politics, it never is.

When one individual can finance an election
while millions of citizens can only vote once,
equality dissolves quietly.

Political access becomes unequal long before laws change.

By the time inequality is visible,
it is already entrenched.

Lessons from History: Russia, China, Hong Kong

The merger of wealth and power follows predictable
patterns.

Russia: From Privatization to Submission

In post-Soviet Russia, rapid privatization created oligarchs
overnight.

At first, wealth dominated politics.
Later, politics reclaimed wealth.

The state did not disappear.
It reasserted control.

Those who aligned survived.
Those who resisted were dismantled.

Oligarchy did not create freedom.
It created vulnerability.

China: Wealth Without Autonomy

In China, wealth exists only conditionally.

Economic elites prosper as long as they serve state priorities.
Political independence is not tolerated.

The result is not oligarchic rule,
but **elite subordination**.

Wealth grows large,
but never sovereign.

Hong Kong: The Mirage of Permanent Privilege

Hong Kong's tycoons believed economic dominance would shield them politically.

They controlled land, housing, infrastructure.
They influenced policy for decades.

When political conditions shifted,
economic power proved insufficient.

Privileges granted by systems can be withdrawn by systems.

The Universal Pattern

Across systems, the pattern is consistent:

1. Wealth concentrates
2. Wealth enters politics

3. Politics adapts to protect wealth
4. Public trust erodes
5. Instability rises
6. Power recentralizes

At no point does oligarchy deliver long-term security to its creators.

It only postpones reckoning.

Why Oligarchy Always Turns Inward

Oligarchy feeds on exclusion.

As protections expand for the few:

- resentment grows among the many
- legitimacy declines
- polarization intensifies

To preserve itself, oligarchy demands more control:

- over media
- over courts
- over information
- over political competition

This accelerates decay.

Eventually, the system must choose:
reform
or repression.

History suggests which option is more common.

America's Unique Risk

America faces a specific danger.

Its institutions are strong enough to delay collapse,
but flexible enough to be captured.

The system can function
while serving fewer and fewer people.

This makes oligarchy harder to detect—and harder to
reverse.

The danger is not sudden authoritarianism.
The danger is **normalized inequality of power**.

The False Comfort of "We're Different"

Every oligarchic system believes it is exceptional.

Exceptional institutions.
Exceptional culture.
Exceptional safeguards.

None have proven immune.

The belief that wealth can safely control politics without
consequences
is not optimism.
It is historical amnesia.

The Moral Inversion

When wealth merges with power, morality inverts.

Rules become obstacles.
Institutions become tools.
Citizens become risks.

Success is no longer measured by contribution,
but by insulation from consequence.

This is the moral failure of oligarchy.

Transition to the Next Question

Chapter 7 establishes the structural danger.

The next question is unavoidable:

If oligarchy is unstable,
and democracy cannot survive unlimited money,
what must be done?

The answer begins with one principle:

Democracy must not be for sale.

Chapter 8 — Democracy Must Not Be for Sale

Campaign Finance, Dark Money, and the Restoration of Political Equality

Democracy is not defined by voting alone.
It is defined by **equal political influence**.

When every citizen has one vote but only a small minority has the power to decide who runs, which ideas are heard, and which laws are written, democracy has already failed—structurally, not rhetorically.

This is not a conspiracy.
It is an outcome.

From "One Person, One Vote" to the Money Amplifier

The core promise of democratic government is political equality.

Not equality of outcome,
but equality of participation and influence.

Modern campaign finance introduced an amplifier into this system: **money**.

Money does not replace votes.
It operates *before* votes matter:

- deciding who can run
- deciding who can be visible
- deciding which issues are amplified
- deciding which issues disappear

When political competition is unequal at the starting line, elections merely ratify inequality.

How Campaign Finance Rewires Political Loyalty

As the cost of elections rises, political accountability shifts.

Candidates no longer answer primarily to voters.
They answer to **funding structures**.

This is not a question of personal morality.
It is a question of systemic incentives.

A political system that requires constant fundraising will inevitably serve those who provide the funds.

Super PACs: Legalized Asymmetry

The emergence of Super PACs represents a structural rupture in democratic design.

They allow:

- theoretical independence
- practical coordination
- unlimited funding
- minimal transparency

Legally, they are separate from candidates.

Functionally, they decide political outcomes.

This is not illegal corruption.
It is **institutionalized inequality of influence**.

Dark Money: Power Without Accountability

The danger of dark money is not merely secrecy.

It is untraceable motivation.

- voters cannot evaluate interests
- policies cannot be held accountable
- trust erodes systematically

Democracy requires visibility.
Dark money depends on invisibility.

When citizens cannot see who is shaping policy,
democratic consent becomes fictional.

The Legal Error: Treating Money as Speech

Equating money with speech is a fundamental democratic
mistake.

Speech is personal expression.
Money is a **force multiplier**.

When money receives unlimited expressive rights,
expression itself ceases to be equal.

This is not censorship.

It is recognition that **voice and amplification are not the same thing**.

No democracy can survive unlimited amplification.

The Social Consequences of Political Inequality

When political influence concentrates, outcomes follow predictably:

- policy tilts toward capital
- long-term public investment declines
- healthcare, education, and housing costs rise
- citizens experience political powerlessness

Public anger is not irrational.
It is a rational response to exclusion.

The danger lies not in anger itself,
but in its misdirection.

Why More Voting Is Not Enough

In a system captured by money, higher turnout alone cannot restore democracy.

If:

- candidate selection is money-controlled
- media visibility is money-driven
- policy formation is money-shaped

Then voting confirms limited choices rather than expands them.

Democratic failure is not apathy.
It is **constrained choice**.

Conditions for Restoring Political Equality

Americalism is explicit:

Without severing the direct pipeline between wealth and power, reform is cosmetic.

At minimum, restoring political equality requires:

1. strict limits on campaign contributions
2. elimination or severe restriction of Super PACs
3. full transparency of political funding
4. public financing options to reduce private dependence

These are not radical proposals.
They are democratic maintenance.

This Is Not Anti-Wealth

Americalism does not oppose success, enterprise, or innovation.

It opposes **purchased sovereignty**.

In a healthy republic:

- wealth may exist

- enterprise may thrive
- innovation may reward

But no private fortune may purchase the direction of the state.

Democracy's Red Line

Democracy does not require consensus.
It requires **equal standing**.

When politics becomes a marketplace, democracy loses its meaning.

Americalism draws a clear boundary:

> Democracy is not a commodity.
> The state is not for sale.
> Citizens are not customers.

Transition

If democracy cannot be sold, then wealth must accept responsibility.

That leads to the next question—one many systems avoid:

Has extreme wealth itself become a moral failure?

Chapter 9 — The Moral Failure of Extreme Wealth

Wealth Without Responsibility, Why Taxation Is Not Punishment, and the American Social Contract Revisited

Extreme wealth is not immoral by definition.
But when wealth becomes detached from responsibility, it becomes dangerous.

This chapter does not argue against success, innovation, or prosperity.
It argues against a condition in which **private accumulation outpaces public obligation**, and in doing so erodes the foundations that made wealth possible in the first place.

That condition now defines modern America.

When Wealth Stops Being a Social Achievement

In a functioning society, wealth reflects contribution.

It may reward:

- innovation
- risk
- labor
- coordination
- leadership

But it remains embedded in a broader system.

Extreme wealth breaks that relationship.

When fortunes grow not through expanded contribution, but through:

- monopoly rents
- financial extraction
- regulatory capture
- political insulation

wealth ceases to be a measure of value creation and becomes a measure of **systemic imbalance**.

This is the point at which wealth loses moral neutrality.

The Disappearance of Reciprocity

Every durable society operates on reciprocity.

Individuals benefit from public goods:

- infrastructure
- legal systems
- security
- education
- stability

In return, they contribute proportionally.

Extreme wealth severs this exchange.

When the wealthiest actors:

- minimize taxation
- externalize costs
- privatize gains
- socialize risks

they remain beneficiaries of the system while withdrawing support for it.

This is not efficiency.
It is **free-riding at scale**.

Why Taxation Is Not Punishment

Taxation is often framed as confiscation or hostility toward success.

This framing is false.

Taxation is **membership due**.

It is the price of participating in a stable, lawful, cooperative society.

Historically, America understood this.

During its strongest periods:

- top marginal tax rates were high
- wealth accumulation was slower
- reinvestment was encouraged
- public trust was stronger

High taxation did not destroy capitalism.
It disciplined it.

Extreme Wealth as a Systemic Risk

Concentrated wealth introduces risks that markets cannot correct:

- political distortion
- social fragmentation
- economic fragility
- democratic erosion

No private actor, regardless of intelligence or intention, should possess the capacity to:

- dominate political agendas
- shape regulatory environments unilaterally
- influence national direction without accountability

This is not a personal failure.
It is a **structural hazard**.

The Myth of Self-Creation

Extreme wealth is often defended by the myth of individual self-creation.

This myth ignores reality.

No fortune is created in isolation.

Every large accumulation depends on:

- public infrastructure
- educated labor
- legal enforcement

- monetary stability
- geopolitical protection

When individuals claim absolute ownership without obligation, they deny the collective foundation of their success.

That denial undermines the legitimacy of wealth itself.

Wealth Without Responsibility Erodes Trust

Trust is the invisible infrastructure of society.

It cannot be bought.
It cannot be coerced.
It must be sustained.

When citizens see:

- elites exempt from rules
- gains privatized and losses shared
- influence bought rather than earned

trust collapses.

Once trust is lost, societies do not become efficient. They become brittle.

Why Redistribution Is the Wrong Word

Americalism does not advocate redistribution as ideology.

It advocates **rebalancing as maintenance**.

Just as infrastructure requires upkeep,
so do economic systems.

Taxation of extreme wealth is not about leveling outcomes.
It is about preventing destabilization.

This is not envy.
It is engineering.

The American Social Contract Revisited

The American social contract was never:
"Anyone who wins owes nothing."

It was:
"Opportunity exists because we build it together."

When wealth grows so large that it exits this contract, the
contract itself weakens.

Reasserting contribution is not radical.
It is conservative in the deepest sense.

It preserves the republic.

The Choice Facing the Wealthy

History is unambiguous.

When elites refuse responsibility:

- public resentment grows
- political instability follows

- reform becomes coercive rather than voluntary

The choice is not whether contribution will occur. The choice is **how**.

Responsibility accepted early preserves dignity. Responsibility resisted invites force.

Moral Failure Is Not About Wealth Size

The moral failure of extreme wealth is not its scale.

It is its **insulation**.

When wealth is shielded from consequence, accountability, and reciprocity, it ceases to be compatible with democracy.

At that point, reform is not punishment. It is necessity.

Transition to the Alternative

Chapters 6–9 have outlined the problem:

- global illusion
- dependency
- power concentration
- democratic capture
- moral detachment

The next question is unavoidable:

What replaces a system that no longer sustains itself?

The answer is not left or right.
It is not ideology.

It is **Americalism**.

Chapter 10 — What Is Americalism?

Beyond Left and Right, Freedom with Responsibility, and a Uniquely American Civic Model

Americalism is not a slogan.
It is not a rebranded ideology.
It is not a compromise between left and right.

Americalism is a **civilizational response** to a system that no longer works.

When political language collapses into tribal labels, when "capitalism" and "socialism" become weapons rather than tools of understanding, societies lose the ability to repair themselves. Americalism emerges from that failure — not to replace democracy, but to restore it.

1. Why the Left–Right Divide No Longer Explains Reality

The dominant political debate in the United States still revolves around an outdated question:
How big should government be?

But America's crisis is no longer about size.
It is about **function**.

The real questions are:

- Who controls political power?
- Who benefits from economic growth?
- Can ordinary citizens still live with dignity?

- Can the nation still maintain its own basic capabilities?

On these questions, both traditional camps fail.

The left often focuses on redistribution while neglecting institutional capacity, production, and trust.
The right speaks of freedom while ignoring extreme power concentration and market capture.

Americalism begins where this debate ends.

2. Defining Americalism

Americalism is a democratic civic framework that places human dignity, shared responsibility, and institutional balance at the center of American political and economic life.

It rests on three non-negotiable principles:

1. **Democracy must not be for sale**
2. **Freedom requires dignity to be meaningful**
3. **Success must carry responsibility**

These are not moral abstractions.
They are design rules for a functioning republic.

3. Freedom With Responsibility — Not Freedom Without Consequence

Americalism does not reject free markets.
It rejects **consequence-free power**.

When "freedom" allows:

- monopolization without accountability,
- profit without reinvestment,
- risk to be externalized onto society,
- political influence to be purchased,

then freedom ceases to be a civic right and becomes a private weapon.

Americalism insists on a simple correction:

> **Freedom must expand together with responsibility.**
>
> This is not restriction.
> It is protection — of democracy, markets, and social stability.

4. Why Americalism Is Not Socialism

Americalism does not advocate state ownership of the economy.
It does not deny private enterprise, innovation, or wealth creation.

The difference is structural:

- Socialism emphasizes **outcome equality**

- Americalism emphasizes **rule integrity**

Americalism does not promise equal results.
It guarantees:
- fair rules,
- unmanipulated institutions,
- protection of basic human dignity.

This is the logic of a **republic**, not a command economy.

5. Why Americalism Rejects Extreme Capitalism

Extreme capitalism assumes markets self-correct regardless of concentration, financialization, or political capture.

Americalism rejects this assumption.

When markets are dominated by oligopolies, detached from production, and fused with political power, they no longer generate prosperity — they extract it.

Americalism does not oppose markets.
It insists that markets:
'

- operate within democratic boundaries,
- respect long-term social stability,
- remain subordinate to public rules.

This is not anti-capitalism.
It is **civilized capitalism**.

6. Americalism as a Civic Model

Americalism is not primarily a policy checklist.
It is a redefinition of citizenship.

Citizens are not:
- passive consumers,
- data points,
- or occasional voters.

Citizens are:

- stewards of institutions,
- participants in shared responsibility,
- guardians of future stability.

Americalism restores citizenship as an **active role**,
not a symbolic one.

7. Why Americalism Is Uniquely American

Americalism is not imported ideology.

It is rooted in America's deepest traditions:

- constitutional limits on power,
- rejection of hereditary privilege,
- civic responsibility,
- community self-governance,
- distrust of concentrated authority.

It revives the original American idea:
a republic, not an empire.

8. The Three Structural Pillars of Americalism (Preview)

Americalism becomes concrete through three institutional pillars, developed in the following chapters:

1. **The Dignity Economy**
— healthcare, education, and housing as foundations of freedom, not market punishments.

2. **Made Local Capability Rebuilding**
— restoring minimum domestic production to anchor prices, skills, and resilience.

3. **Progressive Taxation and Democratic Repair**
— responsibility-based taxation to prevent power concentration and restore institutional trust.

These are not ideological goals.
They are **system repair mechanisms**.

9. Americalism Is Not a Utopia

Americalism does not promise perfection.

It recognizes:
- human fallibility,
- market failure,
- power's tendency to concentrate.

That is precisely why it chooses **institutional design over moral fantasy**.

Americalism is a pragmatic middle-civilization path.

10. From Diagnosis to Construction

The earlier parts of this book exposed:

- the illusion of global outsourcing,
- the rise of oligarchic power,
- the moral failure of extreme wealth.

From this chapter forward, the question changes:

Not *what is broken* — but *how to rebuild.*

Chapter 11 — The Dignity Economy

Why Dignity Is the Foundation of Freedom, and Why Wellbeing Is National Strength

Freedom without dignity is fragile.
It exists in theory but collapses in daily life.

A society may declare itself free, yet if its people live in constant fear of illness, eviction, debt, or collapse, that freedom becomes hollow. It survives only on paper, not in lived experience.

The Dignity Economy begins with a simple recognition:

> **A nation is only as free as the daily lives of its people are stable.**

1. Dignity Is Not Charity

In political discourse, dignity is often misunderstood as compassion, generosity, or moral sentiment. Americalism rejects this framing.

Dignity is not charity.
Dignity is not generosity.
Dignity is not redistribution for its own sake.

Dignity is **infrastructure**.

Just as roads, bridges, and power grids allow an economy to function, dignity allows a society to remain coherent, productive, and democratic.

Without dignity:

- people become desperate,
- decisions become short-term,
- trust erodes,
- politics radicalizes,
- institutions lose legitimacy.

A dignity-less society may still grow economically, but it decays socially.

2. Why Dignity Is the Precondition of Freedom

Freedom requires agency.
Agency requires stability.

A person living one illness away from bankruptcy is not free.
A family one rent increase away from eviction is not free.
A student beginning adult life under crushing debt is not free.

They may vote.
They may speak.
But their choices are constrained by fear.

The Dignity Economy asserts a foundational principle:

Freedom is not the absence of government; freedom is the presence of stability.

This does not weaken liberty.
It makes liberty usable.

3. Healthcare: From Market Punishment to Social Stability

No advanced society can remain stable if access to healthcare is treated primarily as a market transaction.

When healthcare is commodified:

- illness becomes financial catastrophe,
- risk is privatized downward,
- productivity declines,
- social trust collapses.

The Dignity Economy reframes healthcare as:

- a **public stability system**, not a moral benefit,
- a **national resilience mechanism**, not an entitlement,
- a **cost reducer**, not a burden.

Preventive care is cheaper than crisis care.
Universal access is cheaper than mass insecurity.
Healthy citizens are more productive, less fearful, and more civically engaged.

Healthcare is not socialism.
It is **civilizational maintenance**.

4. Education: From Debt Trap to National Investment

Education was once America's greatest equalizer.
It is now one of its most powerful sorting mechanisms.

When education becomes debt-based:

- risk shifts to the young,
- innovation is discouraged,
- talent is wasted,
- social mobility collapses.

A society that finances education through lifelong debt undermines its own future.

The Dignity Economy treats education as:

- **human capital formation**, not consumer purchase,
- **long-term investment**, not private gamble,
- **national strength**, not individual burden.

This does not mean abolishing standards or competition.
It means aligning incentives so that learning builds society rather than enslaving graduates.

5. Housing: Stability Before Speculation

Housing is the physical foundation of dignity.

Without stable shelter:

- families fragment,
- health declines,
- education fails,
- communities dissolve.

When housing is treated primarily as a speculative asset:

- prices detach from wages,
- inequality accelerates,
- cities hollow out,
- social resentment grows.

The Dignity Economy asserts a clear boundary:

Housing must serve life before it serves finance.

This does not eliminate markets.
It restrains financial excess where it destroys social function.

Stable housing anchors:

- family formation,
- workforce participation,
- community continuity,
- democratic trust.

A society that cannot house its people cannot govern itself.

6. Human Wellbeing as National Strength

Traditional power metrics focus on:

- GDP,
- stock indices,
- corporate profits.

These indicators can rise while society weakens.

The Dignity Economy proposes a different measurement of strength:

- health outcomes,
- educational access,
- housing stability,
- civic trust,
- long-term resilience.

A nation with high wellbeing:

- absorbs shocks better,
- resists extremism,
- sustains democracy,
- innovates responsibly.

Wellbeing is not softness.
It is **strategic strength**.

7. The Economic Logic of Dignity

Critics often ask:
"Can we afford dignity?"

Americalism turns the question around:

Can we afford instability?

The costs of indignity include:
- emergency healthcare,
- crime and incarceration,
- political radicalization,
- declining productivity,

- institutional breakdown.

Dignity is not expensive.
Chaos is.

A Dignity Economy does not eliminate markets.
It **reduces friction, lowers risk,** and **extends time horizons**.

8. Why the Dignity Economy Is Not Ideological

The Dignity Economy is not left-wing.
It is not right-wing.

It does not aim to equalize outcomes.
It aims to stabilize foundations.

It does not deny personal responsibility.
It makes responsibility possible.

It does not replace markets.
It civilizes them.

This is not ideology.
It is system repair.

9. Dignity and Democracy Are Inseparable

A population living in fear cannot sustain democracy.

When dignity collapses:

- voters become vulnerable to manipulation,
- anger replaces deliberation,

- demagogues flourish,
- institutions lose legitimacy.

The Dignity Economy is therefore not only social policy.
It is **democratic defense**.

A dignified citizenry is harder to deceive, harder to divide, and harder to dominate.

10. From Dignity to Capability

Dignity alone is not enough.

Stability must be paired with **capability** — the ability of a society to produce, repair, and sustain itself.

This leads to the next pillar of Americalism:

> **Made Local — rebuilding domestic capacity, skills, and resilience.**

Chapter 12 — Made Local: Rebuilding Capability

Why Domestic Production Determines Prices, Labor Stability, and the Future of Democracy

A society's stability is not determined by how much it consumes,
but by whether it can produce, repair, and sustain itself.

Dignity provides the foundation of freedom.
Capability determines whether that foundation can endure.

The third pillar of Americalism is therefore not ideology,
but capacity — and capacity begins with Made Local.

1. The Loss of Capability: When a Society Forgets How to Do Things

Over the past four decades, the United States did not merely outsource factories.
It outsourced skills, systems, standards, and time horizons.

When manufacturing disappeared, the losses were cumulative and structural:
- skilled trades vanished,
- apprenticeship systems collapsed,
- repair ecosystems eroded,
- parts compatibility and industrial standards broke down,
- local supplier networks dissolved.

102

What replaced them was not a higher form of efficiency,
but a fragile, paper-wealth economy.

Today:
- a leaking pipe can take weeks to fix,
- basic electrical work is expensive and inconsistent,
- appliances are cheaper upfront but fail faster,
- infrastructure is "maintained" repeatedly yet deteriorates more rapidly each time.

This is not inefficiency.
It is capability failure.

A society that no longer knows how to make and fix things
cannot remain stable, regardless of GDP.

2. Globalization as a Temporary Fix — Now Fully Exhausted

For a time, global outsourcing functioned as an economic patch.

In the post–Cold War era, under conditions of:
- cheap energy,
- abundant global labor,
- favorable demographics,
- weak environmental enforcement,
- fragmented geopolitics,

the world subsidized American affordability.

That world no longer exists.
- Asia is no longer cheap
- Europe is aging
- Energy is constrained
- Climate costs are unavoidable
- Geopolitics is fractured

Most critically, former production partners are now strategic competitors and system controllers.

What once looked like efficiency was delayed cost.

3. China: From Follower to Structural Controller

China's rise was not accidental.

Over decades, it systematically:

- absorbed outsourced industries,
- replicated and improved technologies,
- captured intermediate manufacturing nodes,
- consolidated upstream and downstream supply chains,
- shaped pricing power and industrial standards.

China moved from *factory of the world*
to controller of industrial bottlenecks.

In many sectors today, China is no longer merely a competitor.
It is a price-setter, supply gatekeeper, and standards influencer.

This is not a moral judgment.

It is a strategic reality.

America traded long-term capability
for short-term price illusion —
and is now constrained by that choice.

4. Manufacturing Loss, Skill Collapse, and the Hidden Driver of Illegal Immigration

One of the most misunderstood debates in American public life is illegal immigration.

It is often framed as:

- a moral failure,
- a border failure,
- or a political failure.

In reality, illegal immigration is largely a structural labor failure —
a symptom of something deeper and far more consequential:

The collapse of domestic manufacturing and the destruction of America's skill ladder.

Illegal immigration did not create this crisis.
It filled the vacuum left behind.

5. What Manufacturing Once Provided — Beyond Jobs

For most of the 20th century, American manufacturing did more than produce goods.
It produced social structure.

Manufacturing provided:

- entry-level technical jobs for non-college workers,
- apprenticeship systems and skill progression,
- stable wages capable of supporting families,
- a clear path from labor to middle-class dignity.

The traditional pathway looked like this:

High school → apprenticeship or shop-floor work → skilled technician → supervisor, owner, or technical specialist

This system absorbed millions of Americans who were not academically elite,
but were technically capable, disciplined, and productive.

It anchored communities.
It stabilized families.
It transmitted skills across generations.

6. What Happened When Manufacturing Left

When large portions of manufacturing were outsourced between the 1980s and early 2000s, the damage extended far beyond factories.

America lost:

- technical entry points,
- skill transmission systems,
- trade schools tied to real production,

- wage structures that rewarded skill over credentials.

In their place emerged:

- low-skill service jobs with no advancement,
- credential inflation and student debt,
- geographic job deserts,
- communities without economic purpose.

This was not merely job loss.
It was capability loss.

7. The Labor Vacuum No One Talks About

Even today, many low- and mid-level jobs still exist in:

- construction,
- agriculture,
- food processing,
- warehousing and logistics,
- residual manufacturing.

But these jobs now suffer from a structural contradiction:

They require labor,
but no longer offer skill progression, dignity, or stability.

As a result:

- local workers avoid them,
- young people are educated away from them,
- training pipelines no longer exist.

This creates a domestic labor vacuum.

8. Illegal Immigration as a Systemic Substitute

In that vacuum, illegal immigration becomes not an accident —
but a systemic substitute.

Employers facing:

- chronic labor shortages,
- tight margins,
- no local skill supply,

turn to the only workforce still willing to accept:

- low wages,
- physical risk,
- minimal protection,
- limited mobility.

Illegal immigration becomes the short-term patch for long-term structural decay.

This is why enforcement alone never works.

You cannot police away an economy
that no longer functions structurally.

9. Why Border Politics Miss the Point

Framing illegal immigration solely as a border issue ignores reality.

As long as:

- domestic capability remains hollow,
- skill ladders remain broken,
- manufacturing remains externalized,

the economic demand for undocumented labor will persist —
regardless of walls, patrols, or rhetoric.

This is not a moral argument.
It is an economic diagnosis.

10. Why Inflation Is Also a Capability Problem

The same structural failure explains inflation.

- Interest rate hikes cannot create plumbers.
- Wage increases cannot manufacture spare parts.
- Monetary policy cannot rebuild skill ecosystems.

Inflation is not primarily about excess money.
It is about missing capability.

Without a domestic production base,
price stability becomes impossible.

11. Why 25% Made Local Changes Everything

The 25% Made Local framework is not protectionism.
It is capability restoration.

By restoring even one-quarter of strategic manufacturing domestically, America rebuilds:

- apprenticeship pathways,
- technical middle-wage jobs,
- skill dignity,
- local labor participation.

As capability returns:

- jobs become trainable again,
- wages stabilize,
- labor regains dignity,
- reliance on undocumented labor naturally declines.

This is demand-side correction, not punishment.

12. Made Local as Social Repair

25% Made Local is therefore not just about trade.

It is about:

- restoring labor sovereignty,
- rebuilding skill-based citizenship,
- repairing community cohesion,
- ending silent exploitation on both sides of the border.

A mature civilization fixes structures —
it does not scapegoat symptoms.

13. The Closed Loop: Capability, Dignity, and Democracy

Dignity requires stability.
Stability requires capability.
Capability requires institutional support.

When capability collapses:

- dignity erodes,
- labor systems distort,
- democracy becomes manipulable,
- extremism rises.

Made Local converts the Dignity Economy from moral aspiration into material reality.

14. From Capability to Responsibility

Once capability is restored, the central question changes.

Not:

Can we produce?
But:
Who bears responsibility for sustaining the system?
That question leads directly to the next pillar of Americalism:

Progressive taxation as civic responsibility.

Core Americalist Principle

A nation that cannot employ its own people with dignity

will eventually import instability.

Rebuilding domestic capability is not
nationalism —
it is social responsibility.

FIGURE 12.1 — Why 25% Made Local Is a Structural Necessity

From Manufacturing Loss to Democratic Fragility

THE STRUCTURAL CHAIN

[Manufacturing Offshoring]
↓
[Skill & Apprenticeship Collapse]
↓
[Domestic Labor Vacuum]
↓
[Reliance on Undocumented Labor]
↓
[Wage Distortion & Social Fracture]
↓
[Political Polarization & Democratic Fragility]

1 Manufacturing Offshoring

- Factories move overseas
- Domestic production ecosystems disappear
- Communities lose economic anchors

Key loss: not just jobs — *capability*

2 Skill & Apprenticeship Collapse

- Entry-level technical jobs vanish
- Trade schools disconnect from real production
- Skill transmission across generations breaks

Result: no ladder from work to dignity

3 Domestic Labor Vacuum

- Jobs still exist (construction, agriculture, food, logistics)
- But they lack:
  - training pathways
  - wage dignity
  - long-term stability

Local workforce exits

4 Reliance on Undocumented Labor

- Employers face labor shortages
- Turn to undocumented workers as a systemic substitute
- Not ideology, not morality — *structural necessity*

Enforcement alone cannot fix this

5 Wage Distortion & Social Fracture

- Shadow labor economy grows

- Wages stagnate
- Communities destabilize
- Immigration debate radicalizes

6 Democratic Fragility

- Economic anxiety fuels extremism
- Trust in institutions erodes
- Politics becomes emotionally manipulable

This is how economic hollowing becomes political crisis

THE TURNING POINT: 25% MADE LOCAL [25% Domestic Production Restored]
↓
[Apprenticeships & Skill Ladders Return]
↓
[Trainable Middle-Wage Jobs]
↓
[Domestic Labor Participation Increases]
↓
[Reduced Dependence on Undocumented Labor]
↓
[Wage Stability & Social Cohesion]
↓
[Democratic Resilience]

WHY 25% (NOT 100%)

Domestic Share	System Effect
< 20%	Extreme fragility
~25%	Price & labor anchoring begins
> 40%	Diminishing returns

25% is the minimum viable capability floor for a modern democracy.

KEY POLICY INSIGHT

Illegal immigration is not primarily a border failure. It is a labor-structure failure caused by four decades of manufacturing offshoring and skill erosion.
A 25% Made Local strategy restores apprenticeship pathways, technical dignity, and domestic labor participation — reducing dependence on undocumented labor naturally, without repression or demonization.

Figure 12.2 POLICY VERSION

Policy Briefing Handout

Why 25% Made Local Is Essential for Labor Stability, Immigration Control, and Democratic Resilience

THE PROBLEM (STRUCTURAL, NOT IDEOLOGICAL)

Illegal immigration is often debated as a border or enforcement issue.
In reality, it is largely a labor-structure failure caused by decades of manufacturing offshoring and skill erosion.

THE STRUCTURAL CHAIN

- Manufacturing offshoring removes domestic production capacity
- Skill ladders and apprenticeships collapse
- Domestic labor exits low-dignity, no-advancement jobs
- Employers face chronic labor shortages
- Undocumented labor becomes a systemic substitute
- Wages distort, communities fracture
- Political polarization intensifies

WHY ENFORCEMENT ALONE FAILS

As long as:

- domestic production remains hollow,
- skill transmission systems are broken,

- dignified work is unavailable,

economic demand for undocumented labor will persist — regardless of border enforcement intensity.

THE SOLUTION: 25% MADE LOCAL

Restoring 25% of essential manufacturing and processing domestically:

- Rebuilds apprenticeship pathways
- Creates trainable middle-wage jobs
- Restores labor dignity
- Draws domestic workers back into essential sectors
- Naturally reduces dependence on undocumented labor

This is demand-side correction, not punishment.

WHY 25% (NOT 100%)

- Achievable within 10 years
- Sufficient to anchor prices and labor markets
- Avoids economic isolation or trade collapse

25% is a structural threshold, not a slogan.

POLICY TAKEAWAY

Illegal immigration is not primarily a border failure.

It is a labor-structure failure caused by the collapse of domestic manufacturing and skill ladders.

A 25% Made Local strategy restores domestic capability and reduces undocumented labor demand naturally, without repression or demonization.

AMERICALIST PRINCIPLE

Fix the structure, and the symptom resolves itself.

FIGURE 12.3 — Structural Diagram

The Hidden Structural Chain: Why 25% Made Local Matters

Manufacturing Loss → Skill Collapse → Labor Vacuum → Illegal Immigration → Democratic Fragility

1 Manufacturing Loss
- Offshoring removes factories and skill ecosystems
- Apprenticeships, shop-floor training, and technical ladders disappear
- Communities lose productive purpose

⬇

2 Skill Collapse
- No entry-level technical jobs for non-college workers

- Trade schools detach from real production
- Work becomes either high-credential or low-dignity

⬇

3 Domestic Labor Vacuum
- Construction, agriculture, food processing, logistics still need labor
- But jobs lack:
  - skill progression
  - wage dignity
  - long-term stability
- Native workforce exits

⬇

4 Illegal Immigration as Structural Substitute
- Employers turn to undocumented labor to survive
- Not because of morality or borders
- But because the domestic labor structure no longer functions

⬇

5 Political & Social Consequences
- Shadow labor economy grows
- Wages stagnate
- Communities fracture
- Immigration debate radicalizes
- Democracy becomes emotionally manipulable

Why Enforcement Alone Always Fails

Because enforcement attacks the symptom, not the structure.

As long as:
- domestic manufacturing is hollow,
- skill ladders are broken,
- dignified work is unavailable,

the demand for undocumented labor will regenerate automatically.

Why 25% Made Local Is the Turning Point

What 25% Does Structurally

Restoring just one-quarter of essential manufacturing:

- Rebuilds apprenticeship pipelines
- Restores skill-based dignity
- Creates trainable middle-wage jobs
- Reconnects education to production
- Draws domestic labor back into the system

This causes:

- $\downarrow$ dependence on undocumented labor
- $\downarrow$ wage distortion
- $\downarrow$ political extremism
- $\uparrow$ social cohesion

Illegal immigration declines naturally — without demonization.

Illegal immigration is not primarily a border failure.

It is a labor-structure failure caused by four decades of manufacturing offshoring and skill erosion.

A 25% Made Local strategy restores apprenticeship pathways, technical dignity, and domestic labor participation — reducing dependence on undocumented labor without repression, fear, or economic self-harm.

One Americalist Principle

A nation that cannot employ its own people with dignity will eventually import instability.

Chapter 13 — Progressive Taxation as Civic Responsibility

How the 1986 Tax Collapse Fueled Extraction, Broke Manufacturing, and Why Repair Now Requires Responsibility at the Top

Every durable society must answer one unavoidable question:

What happens when success is separated from responsibility?

Americalism's answer is not moral outrage and not ideological punishment.
It is institutional repair.

Progressive taxation is not about envy.
It is not about leveling outcomes.
It is not about hostility toward wealth.

It is about **preventing extreme wealth from destroying the economic, social, and democratic systems that made it possible**.

1. The Moment the Balance Was Broken: 1986

The modern American crisis did not begin with globalization.
It began with a policy decision.

In **1986**, the United States collapsed its top marginal income tax rate from **70% to 28%**.

This was not a technical adjustment.
It was a **structural rupture**.

For decades before that moment, high marginal tax rates had served a quiet but essential function:
they **embedded capital inside the domestic economy**.

When extracting profits produced diminishing returns, wealthy individuals and corporations were incentivized to:

- reinvest locally,
- expand production,
- build factories,
- train workers,
- strengthen supply chains,
- think long-term.

High taxes did not destroy capitalism.
They **disciplined it**.

2. From Responsibility to Extraction

The 1986 reform reversed that discipline overnight.

By collapsing the top rate to 28%, the system sent a clear signal:

Extract faster.
Take profits now.
Seek higher returns elsewhere.
Responsibility is no longer required.

The consequences were immediate.

Within the following decade:

- more than **$1 trillion** in additional wealth accumulated at the top,
- corporate profits surged,
- executive compensation exploded,

but **domestic productive investment did not rise proportionally**.
Instead, capital **left**.

3. Globalization Was Not Neutral — It Was Incentive-Driven

What followed is often described as "globalization."

That description is incomplete.

What actually occurred was **tax-engineered capital flight**, later justified by globalization rhetoric.

Freed from responsibility, capital sought:

- cheaper labor,
- weaker regulations,
- externalized environmental costs,
- higher short-term returns.

Manufacturing was not gradually adjusted.
It was **abandoned**.

This was not inevitable technological progress.
It was an incentive failure.

4. The Manufacturing Collapse and the China Transfer

As Western capital exited, entire industrial ecosystems collapsed:

- skilled labor pipelines disappeared,
- local standards dissolved,
- repair networks vanished,
- supply chains fragmented.

The American middle class did not fail.
It was **disconnected** from production.

China did not "steal" manufacturing.
It **received it**.

Western capital transferred:

- machinery,
- know-how,
- supply chains,
- industrial scale,

to a system willing to absorb them.

China began as a follower.
Then a competitor.
Now, in many sectors, a **structural controller** of prices, standards, and supply bottlenecks.

This was not a geopolitical accident.
It was the downstream consequence of Western tax and investment choices.

5. The Social Cost: Middle-Class Collapse and Democratic Erosion

The consequences unfolded predictably.

As manufacturing disappeared:

- middle-class jobs vanished,
- wages stagnated,
- communities hollowed out,
- regional economies collapsed.

The Rust Belt became the Iron Strip.

With economic collapse came:

- despair,
- political radicalization,
- opioid and drug epidemics,
- loss of institutional trust,
- erosion of democratic norms.

This was not cultural failure.
It was **economic abandonment**.

A society that removes responsibility from capital eventually transfers the cost to its people.

6. National Security: The Bill Comes Due

What began as a tax decision became a strategic liability.

By surrendering manufacturing capacity, the United States:

- lost control of critical supply chains,
- became dependent on strategic competitors,

- weakened industrial mobilization capacity,
- compromised economic sovereignty.

Shortages of semiconductors, medical supplies, and energy-adjacent components are not anomalies.

They are the **invoice** for four decades of extraction.

7. The Road Not Taken — and Why Repair Is Still Necessary

This collapse was not inevitable.

Had the 70% marginal rate remained:

- capital flight would have been slower,
- offshoring would have been selective,
- manufacturing loss would have been manageable,
- skills erosion could have been repaired,
- globalization would have occurred **with guardrails**.

Instead, removing responsibility at the exact moment globalization expanded opportunity turned adjustment into collapse.

Because the damage accumulated over **forty years**, repair cannot be symbolic.

8. Why Progressive Taxation Must Be Restored — and Strengthened

Americalism therefore argues:

Repair must match the scale and duration of the harm.
Returning merely to pre-1986 norms is insufficient.

The system now requires:

• **progressive marginal income taxes rising toward 70–80% at the highest brackets**, and

• **a wealth tax on net worth above $10 million**, escalating with scale.

This is not punishment.
It is **structural correction**.

9. Why a Wealth Tax Is Now Unavoidable

Extreme wealth today is no longer primarily earned income.

It is:

• accumulated,
• inherited,
• financialized,
• shielded from realization,
• converted into political influence.

Without a wealth tax:

• inequality becomes permanent,
• oligarchy consolidates,
• democracy weakens irreversibly.

A wealth tax above $10 million:

- targets concentration, not success,
- prevents dynastic lock-in,
- returns idle capital to productive circulation,
- funds dignity and capability rebuilding.

10. Why Top Rates Must Reach 80%

High marginal rates do not confiscate wealth.
They **change behavior**.

At extreme income levels:

- extraction becomes irrational,
- reinvestment becomes attractive,
- hoarding loses appeal,
- political rent-seeking declines.

This was proven during America's strongest era.

High top rates do not stop people from becoming rich.
They stop people from becoming **dangerously powerful**.

11. Taxation as Democratic Defense

When wealth concentrates without obligation, democracy becomes an auction.

Progressive taxation:

- reduces surplus capital available for political capture,

- restores balance between citizens and money,
- protects institutions from oligarch dominance.

This is not class warfare.
It is **republican self-preservation**.

12. Repair, Not Revenge

Americalism does not seek revenge for past mistakes.

It seeks **repair proportional to damage**.

For forty years:

- responsibility was removed from capital,
- extraction replaced production,
- wealth overwhelmed democracy.

Now responsibility must return.
Progressive taxation and wealth taxation are not ideological demands.
They are **civilizational maintenance**.

13. The Choice Ahead

America now faces two paths:

1. Preserve the post-1986 system
→ permanent oligarchy, fragile democracy, declining capability

2. Restore responsibility to success

→ rebuilt production, renewed middle class, resilient democracy

Americalism chooses the second.
Not because it is radical —
but because **the alternative has already failed**

Chapter 14 — Inflation Is Not a Monetary Problem, but a Capability Problem

I. Why Traditional Inflation Explanations No Longer Work

When inflation rises, the dominant explanation is almost always the same:

There is too much money.

The standard response follows automatically:

- central banks raise interest rates,
- credit tightens,
- demand is suppressed.

Yet reality keeps contradicting this logic:

- interest rates rise, but housing costs keep climbing;
- interest rates rise, but food prices remain elevated;
- interest rates rise, but repair, healthcare, and service costs continue to increase.

This is not a failure of execution.
It is a failure of diagnosis.

Today's inflation is no longer a cyclical monetary phenomenon.
It is the price signal of structural capability erosion.

II. When a Society Loses the Ability to Do Things, Prices Can Only Rise

Inflation ultimately reflects whether a society can:

- produce,
- repair,
- maintain,
- supply,
- and absorb shocks.

For most of the twentieth century, the United States could domestically produce:
- plumbing components,
- electrical systems,
- appliances,
- construction materials,
- agricultural equipment.

It also possessed:

- skilled trades,
- local repair networks,
- interchangeable parts systems.

When capability exists, prices have an anchor.

III. Manufacturing Hollowing: The First Layer of Inflation

Over the past forty years, the United States systematically outsourced its manufacturing capacity.

The consequences were cumulative:

- dependence on imports,
- fragmented standards,
- broken skill transmission,
- longer repair cycles,
- higher replacement costs.

Today, a simple repair often:

- takes weeks,
- costs more than replacement,
- results in full disposal rather than maintenance.

Low quality is no longer cheap.
It is the most expensive option over time.

IV. Interest Rates Cannot Create Capability

Monetary policy can only do one thing:

Suppress demand.

It cannot:

- train electricians,
- develop welders,
- build factories,
- or restore supply chains.

When capability is missing, suppressing demand only increases social pain without stabilizing prices.

V. Industrialized Agriculture: A Hidden Driver of Inflation

Among all forms of capability erosion, agriculture is the most underestimated—and the most dangerous.

The core purpose of agriculture is not profit maximization. It is stable nourishment of communities.

That purpose has been abandoned.

VI. The Subsidy Illusion: Money That Never Reaches Farmers

The United States spends tens of billions of dollars annually on agricultural subsidies, yet food prices keep rising.

The reason is simple:

The money does not reach farmers.

Under the label of "agriculture," subsidies concentrate in oligopolistic systems:

- seed corporations,
- chemical and pesticide firms,
- machinery manufacturers,
- large commodity traders and distributors.

Farmers carry the risk.
Corporations capture the margin.
Consumers pay higher prices.

VII. Prices Are Set by Channels, Not by Farmers

In the modern food system:

- farmers do not set prices;
- procurement prices are dictated by dominant buyers;
- retail prices are controlled by commercial distribution systems.

Farmers are squeezed between:

- rising input costs,
- and suppressed purchase prices.

This is not a free market.
It is structural compression.

VIII. When Small Farmers Disappear, Prices Lose Their Stabilizer

History shows repeatedly:

Price stability comes from decentralization, not scale.

Where local farmers are numerous:

- shocks are absorbed,
- prices are harder to manipulate,
- communities self-correct.

When small farmers disappear:

- minor disruptions become systemic price spikes,
- "temporary" inflation becomes permanent,
- food prices lose any downward elasticity.

IX. Local Farmers × Local Tables: A Forgotten Anti-Inflation Mechanism

Americalism emphasizes a neglected principle:

> Price stability comes from proximity, not volume.

- local farmers → local markets
- community farms → community tables
- backyard gardens → household nutrition

Short supply chains mean:

- lower transport costs,
- greater price flexibility,
- stronger food security.

This is not nostalgia.
It is capability economics.

X. The Tariff Fallacy: Why Blanket Tariffs Accelerate Inflation

One of the most dangerous misunderstandings in current U.S. policy debates is the belief that general tariffs on all countries will automatically rebuild domestic industry.

They will not.

When domestic capability has already been hollowed out, across-the-board tariffs do the opposite:

- they immediately raise prices;

- they worsen affordability;
- they strain already fragile supply chains.

The United States still depends heavily on imported goods and raw materials.
Imposing sudden, universal tariffs without domestic alternatives simply transfers costs to consumers.

This is not industrial rebuilding.
It is inflationary self-harm.

XI. The Only Viable Path: Import Quotas Combined with Targeted Tariffs

Americalism does not reject tariffs.
It rejects tariffs without industrial policy.

The effective approach is structural, not ideological:

Import quotas + targeted tariffs.
- Quotas create guaranteed domestic market space.
- Tariffs create predictable long-term investment returns.

The objective is not immediate import elimination, but a 10-year transition toward restoring 25% of essential and basic goods production domestically.

Only when capacity returns:
- prices stabilize,
- investment becomes rational,
- skills rebuild,
- inflation subsides structurally.

XII. Regulation Must Be Rebuilt, Not Weaponized

Many current food and agricultural regulations were designed for large-scale industrial systems.

The result:
- small farmers are excluded,
- local slaughter becomes infeasible,
- small-scale livestock and diversified farming cannot survive.

Americalism advocates:
- scale-based regulation,
- proportional risk standards,
- realistic oversight instead of bureaucratic templates.

Otherwise, regulation becomes an oligarchic moat.

XIII. Agricultural Capability Is National Security

A nation unable to supply its own basic food reliably is not secure.

Food is not an ordinary commodity.
It is strategic capacity.

XIV. Conclusion: Inflation Is the Price Signal of Capability Loss

The Americalist conclusion is clear:
- today's inflation is not accidental;

- it is the cumulative result of long-term capability erosion.

The solution is not:
- ever-higher interest rates,
- temporary subsidies,
- or indiscriminate tariffs.

The solution is:
- rebuilding manufacturing capacity,
- restoring agricultural capability,
- reconstructing local skills,
- and re-anchoring community supply systems.

When capability returns, prices stabilize naturally.

Chapter 15 Climate, Speed, and Civilization: Why the Real Crisis Is Not Emissions, but Loss of Control

I. The Crisis Is Not Climate Alone — It Is a Civilization Losing Control

When climate change is discussed, it is often reduced to numbers:
degrees, targets, deadlines.

But civilizations do not collapse because a thermometer moves.
They collapse when **complex systems exceed their capacity to adapt**.

The real question before humanity is not whether the Earth survives —
the planet has endured far greater disruptions.

The question is whether **human civilization**, with its cities, food systems, supply chains, public health, and democratic institutions, can continue to function **within a stable operating range**.

Climate change is not an isolated environmental issue.
It is a **signal** that the economic and production systems driving civilization have exceeded sustainable limits.

This chapter argues that the true driver of the climate crisis is not consumption alone, but **speed** —

the uncontrolled acceleration of capital, production, logistics, and extraction.

II. Speed: The Most Dangerous and Least Recognized Form of Pollution

Over the last forty years, global capitalism has not merely grown —
it has **accelerated**.

- Capital circulates faster than societies can absorb.
- Supply chains stretch across continents.
- Products are designed for replacement, not durability.
- Food is engineered for shelf life, not human health.
- Agriculture is optimized for volume, not communities.

This acceleration creates a fatal illusion:
that efficiency can substitute for stability.

In reality, when economic speed exceeds ecological, social, and biological limits, efficiency becomes destructive.

Manufacturing alone accounts for roughly **38% of global CO_2 emissions**, with long-distance shipping contributing another **3–4%**.
But emissions are only the visible symptom.

The deeper damage lies in:

- Fragile supply chains

142

- Collapsing local economies
- Rising health costs
- Political radicalization
- Democratic erosion

Climate change is not the cause —
it is the **feedback loop**.

III. The Goal Is Not Micro-Reductions, but Stable Climate Control

It is essential to clarify a critical point.

The objective of climate policy is **not** to "reduce the warming trajectory by 0.1–0.2°C" through marginal adjustments.

The real objective is to **stabilize global warming within a manageable range — approximately 1–2°C — where civilization can continue to function, adapt, and repair itself**.

This is not a scientific abstraction.
It is a civilizational requirement.

Beyond this range:

- Agricultural zones destabilize
- Food prices become volatile
- Infrastructure fails under stress
- Health systems overload
- Political systems fracture

Climate policy, therefore, must focus on **structural stability**, not symbolic targets.

IV. Why "25% Made Local" Is a Structural Climate Solution

Most climate strategies rely on:

- Costly technological transitions
- Carbon trading mechanisms
- Behavioral micromanagement
- Massive new investments

While not useless, these approaches avoid the core structural issue:
overextended global production systems.

The "25% Made Local" framework proposes a simpler and more natural correction:

Restore approximately 25% of essential manufacturing and production to local or regional economies.

This is not isolationism.
It is **system rebalancing**.

The effects are structural:

- Shorter supply chains
- Lower transport emissions
- Reduced overproduction
- Higher product durability
- Stronger local employment
- Greater resilience to shocks

Emissions decline not because people are forced to consume less,
but because **the system itself slows down**.

V. Industrial Agriculture: The Overlooked Climate and Health Crisis

If manufacturing exposes the cost of distance,
industrial agriculture exposes the cost of disconnection.

Modern agriculture has been transformed into a
financialized, chemical-dependent system detached from
community needs.

In the United States:

- Billions in agricultural subsidies rarely reach farmers
- Capital flows instead to seed monopolies, chemical producers, machinery giants
- Food prices are controlled by commercial channels, not producers
- Farmers operate with shrinking margins and rising debt

The result is a paradox:

- Cheap food that is nutritionally poor
- High output with low resilience
- Subsidized systems that still fail farmers

Processed food has become one of the **largest contributors to obesity, diabetes, and chronic disease** in America.

This is not a lifestyle failure.
It is a **systemic supply failure**.

VI. Reconnecting Land, Food, and Community

A sustainable agricultural system is not defined by scale alone,
but by its relationship to human health and local ecosystems.

A repaired system must:

- Support local and regional farmers
- Encourage farm-to-table supply chains
- Allow small-scale livestock and diversified farming under realistic safety standards
- Enable local slaughter, processing, and distribution
- Promote community farming, urban agriculture, and household food production

This is not romanticism.
It is **civilizational maintenance**.

When food systems serve communities instead of financial velocity:

- Health costs decline
- Emissions fall
- Rural economies stabilize
- Democratic trust strengthens

VII. Taxation as the Civilizational Brake

Climate breakdown is not evenly distributed responsibility.
It is driven disproportionately by **extreme capital concentration and velocity**.

After the drastic reduction of top marginal tax rates
beginning in the mid-1980s, capital behavior changed
fundamentally:

- Investment shifted overseas
- Manufacturing hollowed out
- Agriculture industrialized
- Financial extraction replaced productive
reinvestment

Restoring progressive taxation is not punishment.
It is **system correction**.

High progressive taxes and wealth taxes function as:

- A brake on reckless capital speed
- An incentive for long-term local investment
- A stabilizer for economic and social systems

Taxation is not redistribution alone —
it is **economic engineering for stability**.

VIII. Slowing Down Is Not Decline — It Is Maturity

A mature civilization does not maximize speed.
It maximizes durability.

Stability, repairability, and continuity are higher
achievements than endless growth.

A slower system:

- Produces less waste
- Emits less carbon
- Reduces health crises

- Preserves democratic capacity

This is not sacrifice.
It is **civilizational intelligence**.

IX. Conclusion: Climate Policy Is a Choice About Civilization

Climate change is not an external enemy.
It is the consequence of how we organize production, food, wealth, and power.

If humanity continues to operate a system built on extraction and speed, no technology will save it.

But if we choose:

- Local over excessive global
- Health over cheapness
- Responsibility over accumulation
- Stability over acceleration

Then civilization can remain **within a stable operating range**, capable of adaptation and renewal.

That is the true meaning of climate action.

Not austerity.
Not fear.
But **structural balance**.

Chapter 16   A New Declaration of Interdependence: Why No One Can Be Left Behind

I. From Radical Individualism to Shared Responsibility

America was built on individual freedom.
But freedom was never meant to mean abandonment.

At its best, the American tradition understood a deeper truth:
that liberty survives only when people are strong enough to exercise it.

Over time, this truth was distorted.
Individualism hardened into isolation.
Responsibility was reframed as weakness.
Care was dismissed as dependency.

The result was a dangerous illusion:
that a society could thrive while leaving millions behind.

History proves otherwise.

Civilizations do not collapse because they care too much.
They collapse because they abandon too many.

II. Interdependence Is Not Weakness — It Is Reality

No human being is self-made.

No success exists in isolation.
No wealth is created without a social foundation.

Every life depends on:

- shared infrastructure,
- public safety,
- legal systems,
- education,
- healthcare,
- and the labor of others.

Interdependence is not a political philosophy.
It is a fact of human existence.

Denying it does not create strength —
it creates fragility.

A society that refuses to acknowledge
interdependence
eventually pays for it through instability, crime,
illness, resentment, and collapse.

III. No One Should Be Left Behind — Not as Charity, but as Justice

Americalism rests on a simple, non-negotiable principle:

No one should be left behind.

Not children.
Not the homeless.
Not people with disabilities.
Not those who fall ill.
Not those who lose work.

Not those born into disadvantage.

This does not mean equal outcomes.
It means **guaranteed dignity**.

A civilized society must ensure that every person has:

- food sufficient for health,
- shelter sufficient for safety,
- healthcare sufficient for survival,
- education sufficient for participation,
- and support sufficient for dignity.

These are not luxuries.
They are the minimum conditions for a free society to function.

IV. Children: The Measure of a Civilization's Honesty

Children are not responsible for the system they inherit.

Yet they bear its consequences more than anyone else.

A society that allows children to:

- grow up hungry,
- lack medical care,
- live without stable housing,
- inherit debt instead of opportunity,

has already failed its future.

Investing in children is not social policy.
It is **civilizational preservation**.

Every dollar withheld from children today
returns as social cost tomorrow — multiplied.

V. Homelessness Is Not a Moral Failure — It Is a System Failure

Homelessness is often treated as an individual flaw.
In reality, it is a structural breakdown.

People do not choose:

- untreated mental illness,
- unaffordable housing,
- medical bankruptcy,
- or economic displacement.

A society capable of generating immense wealth
but incapable of guaranteeing basic shelter
is not efficient — it is disordered.

Providing housing stability is not permissiveness.
It is **restoring order**.

No democracy remains stable when large segments of
its population
are pushed outside the social contract.

VI. Disability and Hardship: Dignity Must Not Be Conditional

Disability is not marginal.
Hardship is not rare.

Any human being can become disabled.

Any family can face crisis.
Any worker can be displaced.

A society that conditions dignity on productivity
creates fear instead of loyalty.

Americalism rejects this logic.

Support for people with disabilities and those in hardship
is not dependency —
it is **mutual insurance for a human society**.

When people know they will not be abandoned,
they contribute more, trust more, and fear less.

VII. Basic Living Security as the Foundation of Freedom

Freedom cannot exist on the edge of survival.

People who are:

- hungry,
- sick,
- homeless,
- or desperate,

are not free — they are vulnerable.

Basic living security does not eliminate freedom.
It **enables it**.

By ensuring a floor beneath every life,
society allows people to take risks, innovate, work,
and participate.

This is not generosity.
It is **structural necessity**.

VIII. Interdependence Is How Societies Rise — and How They Survive

Every great civilization understood this truth:
that shared responsibility is the price of continuity.

Empires that glorified extraction fell.
Societies that preserved balance endured.

Americalism does not reject freedom.
It completes it.

Freedom without responsibility is chaos.
Responsibility without freedom is tyranny.

Interdependence is the bridge between them.

IX. Conclusion: A Republic Worth Belonging To

A nation is not defined by how it rewards the strongest,
but by how it treats the most vulnerable.

When no one is left behind:

- democracy stabilizes,
- trust returns,
- violence declines,
- and the future becomes imaginable again.

This is not idealism.
It is realism grounded in history.

A society that rises together
stands longer.

A society that abandons its own
eventually collapses inward.

Americalism chooses the harder path —
because it is the only sustainable one.

No one should be left behind.
Not because we are generous —
but because we are one society.

Chapter 17 Protecting Democracy Is the Only Way to Protect Wealth

A Final Warning to America's Oligarchs

I. When Wealth Merges with Power, the Real Danger Begins

History has never condemned wealth itself.
The true danger begins when wealth seeks to **possess political power**.

When a small group of the extremely wealthy comes to believe that:

- rules can be purchased,
- laws can be bypassed,
- elections can be invested in,
- and power can be privatized,

a republic ceases to be a republic
and begins its slide into **oligarchy**.

This is not a moral judgment.
It is a structural law of politics.

II. The "Just Business" Illusion: When Politics Becomes Uncalculable

Many wealthy actors still operate under an outdated assumption:

"Business is business. Politics is just another risk variable."

This logic collapses once democracy begins to erode.

When power rises above rules,
politics stops being calculable risk
and becomes **arbitrary discretion**.

In such a system:

- markets no longer decide outcomes,
- investment logic breaks down,
- success depends on loyalty, access, posture, and favor.

This is no longer capitalism.
It is **dependency economics**.

No rational capital can survive long
in a system where outcomes are no longer predictable.

III. History Is Unforgiving: Lessons from Russia, China, and Hong Kong

Russia

Oligarchs believed supporting centralized power would buy security.
Instead, they learned:

- property could be seized overnight,
- wealth became a political bargaining chip,

- • safety depended on personal loyalty,
- • children had to bind their futures to the regime.

China

Entrepreneurs discovered that once politics dominates law, property rights become conditional.
Wealth exists at the pleasure of power, not under protection of rules.

Hong Kong

Capital chose accommodation, hoping stability would follow.
What followed instead was:

- • the collapse of rule of law,
- • the evaporation of institutional trust,
- • rapid devaluation of wealth.

**Oligarchs do not win in authoritarian systems.
They are eventually consumed by them.**

IV. You Think You Are Using Power — You Are Training It

Every time money is used to bend politics,
it appears to be a transaction.

In reality, it is **training power to bypass rules**.

Each exception teaches authority one lesson:
rules are optional.

And once power learns this,
it does not relearn restraint.

When the system later seeks a sacrifice,
it will not hesitate.
It will choose the most visible,
most concentrated,
most symbolic wealth.

Power never remembers allies.
But it never forgets
who taught it how to act without limits.

V. When Democracy Falls, Wealth Loses Safety First

For wealth, the most important factor has never been low
taxes.
It has always been:

- stable property rights,
- reliable law,
- institutional predictability,
- family security.

Democracy's greatest value is not efficiency.
It is **predictability**.

When democracy erodes:

- law becomes selectively enforced,
- taxation becomes political punishment,
- wealth becomes leverage,
- families lose control over their future.

This is not wealth protection.

It is placing wealth at the mercy of power's mood.

VI. Populism Will Not Protect You

Some elites believe:

-       fueling social anger,
-       amplifying culture wars,
-       redirecting resentment,

will shield them from accountability.

This is a fatal miscalculation.

History is clear:
populism never burns precisely.

Once unleashed, it seeks visible targets.
Concentrated wealth eventually becomes one of them.

VII. The Real Enemy of Legacy Is Not Tax — It Is Disorder

For those who genuinely care about family legacy,
the greatest threat is not taxation.

It is institutional collapse.

Taxes are predictable costs.
Political disorder is an uncontrollable catastrophe.

A family that pays taxes under democracy
retains:

-       clear ownership,

- lawful inheritance,
- independence for future generations.

In a system where power overrides law,
no wealth truly belongs to the next generation.

Wealth survives across generations only under rules.

VIII. America Was Safe Because It Limited Power

America's long prosperity did not come from favoring the rich.
It came from **limiting power for everyone**.

The Constitution, rule of law, independent courts, free media —
these were not obstacles to wealth,
but the insurance policy that allowed wealth to endure.

Weakening these institutions does not liberate capital.
It **removes its foundation**.

IX. The Americalist Choice for the Wealthy

Americalism is not anti-wealth.
It is not anti-success.
It is not anti-enterprise.

It presents a choice grounded in reality.

Path One:

Short-Term Power × Long-Term Insecurity

- purchase influence,

- manipulate institutions,
- evade responsibility.

Outcome:

- collapsing rules,
- politicized wealth,
- unpredictable futures,
- family vulnerability.

Path Two:

Responsibility × Civilizational Security

- accept fair taxation,
- exit political transactions,
- support democratic repair,
- restore rule-based order.

Outcome:

- stable law,
- restored trust,
- secure inheritance,
- independent future generations.

X. America's "Exception" Is Not Permanent

America was not immune by nature.
It was protected by institutions.

Institutions survive only through maintenance.

When elites choose transactions over institutions,
America's exceptional stability disappears.

No nation survives on inertia
after its rules are hollowed out.

XI. Conclusion: A Warning — and an Invitation

This chapter is not an accusation.
Not a threat.
Not a moral lecture.

It is a clear reminder:

> **Your wealth does not need authoritarian
> power to survive.
> It only needs democracy to continue existing.**

> Choose democracy,
> and you protect not only the country,
> but your name, your family, and your future.

Destroy democracy — there are no winners.
Defend democracy — and legacy becomes possible

Chapter 18   The Choice Before Us
Managed Decline or Deliberate Repair

I. History Does Not Ask for Permission

History does not announce itself politely.
It does not wait for consensus.
It does not pause for comfort.

History moves when conditions converge.
America has reached such a moment.

Not because it is weak,
but because it has delayed repair too long
while believing delay itself was stability.

What lies ahead is not fate.
It is choice.

II. Managed Decline: The Path of Evasion

The first path is familiar, quiet, and politically convenient.

It is the path of **managed decline**.

Under this path:

- inequality continues to widen,
- production capability continues to erode,
- democracy weakens incrementally,

- public trust decays slowly,
- social tension is "managed," not resolved.

Life goes on.
Markets fluctuate.
Elections repeat.
Nothing collapses dramatically.

But nothing heals.

Managed decline does not feel like failure.
It feels like **normalization of loss**.

This path always ends the same way:
not in sudden catastrophe,
but in irreversible diminishment.

III. The Cost of Doing Nothing Is Not Zero

Many believe inaction is neutral.

It is not.

Every year without reform:

- skills disappear,
- communities hollow out,
- institutions lose legitimacy,
- cynicism deepens,
- future options narrow.

In complex systems, delay is not preservation.
It is erosion.

By the time collapse becomes visible,

repair is no longer possible at scale.

IV. Deliberate Repair: The Harder, Necessary Path

The second path is deliberate repair.

It is not revolutionary.
It is restorative.

Deliberate repair means:

- rebuilding production capacity,
- restoring democratic boundaries,
- rebalancing wealth and responsibility,
- stabilizing the foundations of daily life.

It is slower than slogans,
harder than denial,
and politically more demanding than distraction.

But it is the only path that preserves a functioning
civilization.

V. Repair Is Not Regression

Repair is often attacked as nostalgia.

This is a misunderstanding.

Deliberate repair does not mean returning to the past.
It means restoring **capability**.

A society that cannot:

- make essential goods,
- feed itself reliably,
- care for its people,
- govern without corruption,

is not advanced — no matter how wealthy it appears.

Repair is forward-looking realism.

VI. What Happens If America Acts

If America chooses deliberate repair:

- inflation stabilizes structurally,
- supply chains shorten and strengthen,
- communities regain purpose,
- democratic legitimacy recovers,
- climate pressures ease through balance

rather than austerity.

This does not require perfection.
It requires direction.

Civilizations recover not through purity,
but through alignment.

VII. What Happens If America Does Not

If America continues on the path of evasion:

- economic volatility becomes permanent,
- democratic norms degrade further,
- political conflict intensifies,
- external dependence deepens,

- internal cohesion fractures.

Eventually, repair becomes impossible without rupture.

History offers no exceptions to this pattern.

VIII. This Is Not Left vs. Right

This choice is not ideological.

It is structural.

It is not capitalism versus socialism.
It is **function versus breakdown**.

Every society that survived understood this distinction.
Every society that collapsed ignored it.

IX. The Responsibility of This Generation

Every generation inherits a system.
Some improve it.
Some exhaust it.
Some pass it on broken.

This generation will be remembered for one decision:
whether it chose convenience,
or responsibility.

The future will not ask what slogans were shouted.
It will ask whether institutions still worked.

X. A Future Worth Building

America can still choose coherence over chaos,
repair over denial,
dignity over extraction.

That future will not be perfect.
But it will be stable.
And stability is the foundation of freedom.

No society remains free
once instability becomes permanent.

XI. Final Words

This book is not a warning of collapse.
It is an argument for repair.

Not dramatic change,
but necessary change.

Not ideological victory,
but civilizational continuity.

The choice before America is simple —
though not easy:

**Managed decline,
or deliberate repair.**

History will record the answer.

Epilogue

The Human Horizon

Why the System Must Serve the Human

Every system is a tool.
Every economy is a structure.
Every institution is a means, not an end.

When systems forget this, they begin to consume the very people they were meant to serve.

History shows a consistent pattern:
civilizations do not fail because they lack complexity,
they fail because they lose purpose.

Markets without ethics become extraction machines.
States without restraint become instruments of fear.
Technology without direction accelerates harm faster than good.

The human being must remain the reference point.

Not efficiency alone.
Not growth alone.
Not power alone.

But **human dignity, wellbeing, and continuity**.

Any system that cannot protect these ultimately destroys itself.

Why America Can Still Rise

America's strength has never been perfection.
It has been **self-correction**.

The United States has repeatedly demonstrated an unusual
capacity:
to confront failure,
to reform institutions,
and to rebuild legitimacy after crisis.

That capacity has not disappeared.

What has weakened is not the country's potential,
but its willingness to face structural truth.

America can still rise because:

- its institutions are damaged, not destroyed,
- its people are divided, not defeated,
- its productive capacity is weakened, not erased,
- its democratic foundation is strained, not gone.

Repair remains possible — but not indefinitely.

History offers windows, not guarantees.

Why Dignity Comes First

Dignity is not a moral luxury.
It is a structural requirement.

A society that denies dignity creates:

- instability,
- resentment,
- illness,
- violence,
- and distrust.

A society that guarantees dignity creates:

- resilience,
- cooperation,
- long-term growth,
- and democratic legitimacy.

Dignity does not eliminate responsibility.
It makes responsibility sustainable.

Dignity is not the opposite of freedom.
It is the condition that makes freedom real.

When dignity is protected, societies endure.
When it is sacrificed, systems unravel.

The Human Horizon

The future will not be defined by ideology,
but by alignment with human limits.

Climate.
Health.
Social cohesion.
Institutional trust.
Productive balance.

These are not political talking points.

They are **civilizational constraints**.

The human horizon is the boundary within which
civilization can remain stable.
Beyond it, complexity collapses into chaos.

This book argues for one simple principle:

> **Systems must be redesigned to serve the
> human —**
> **or they will eventually fail the human, and
> themselves.**

America still has time.
But time is no longer abundant.

About the Author

ButterflyMan
Independent Thinker | Writer | Observer of Systems

ButterflyMan is an independent thinker and writer focused on the intersection of political economy, manufacturing, democracy, and human dignity.

This work does not seek to found a movement, claim leadership, or prescribe uniform action.
It offers a framework — analytical, historical, and ethical — for individuals, communities, policymakers, and institutions to examine their own roles and responsibilities.

Change, if it comes, will come through many hands.

The author's role is to illuminate structure, risk, and possibility —
and to invite others to decide what they will do with that understanding.

Appendix A — The 25% Made Local in 10 Years Framework

How Structural Rebalancing Restores Stability, Democracy, and Resilience

Core Principle

A nation cannot maintain price stability, social cohesion, or democratic legitimacy if it produces too little of what it consumes.

Inflation, supply fragility, and political instability are not monetary accidents — they are symptoms of **capability loss**.

The **25% Made Local framework** establishes a minimum threshold of domestic and regional production required for systemic stability.

Why 25%?
- **Below 20%**:
  Supply chains remain fragile; prices are externally dictated.
- **Around 25%**:
  Domestic capacity begins to anchor prices and restore resilience.
- **Above 40%**:
  Returns diminish; excessive localization risks inefficiency.

25% is not autarky — it is **strategic balance**.

10-Year Phased Target

Year	Made Local Share
1	2.5%
3	7.5%
5	12.5%
7	17.5%
10	25%

Coverage Areas

- Manufacturing (textiles, appliances, construction materials, components)
- Agriculture & food processing
- Medical and pharmaceutical supply
- Energy-adjacent and critical inputs

Policy Tools

- Progressive tax incentives for local production
- Smart tariffs on predatory or dumping imports
- Public procurement priority for compliant firms
- Workforce training and regional industrial zones
- Credit access for small and medium producers

Expected Outcomes
- Structural inflation control (not rate-dependent)
- Shorter supply chains → lower volatility
- Community job restoration
- National security reinforcement
- Reduced long-term fiscal pressure

Intellectual Origin

This framework draws from:
- **Made Local** theory
- **2510.org** structural production research
- *The Philosophy of the Future of Manufacturing* (Pan Pan)

It is not protectionism — it is **system repair**.

Appendix B — Policy Summary for Lawmakers

Restoring Democratic Balance and Economic Stability

(Non-partisan, Executive-Readable)

I. The Problem

The United States faces a **compound structural crisis**:

- Inflation driven by capacity loss, not demand excess
- Wealth concentration undermining democratic legitimacy
- Deindustrialization threatening national security
- Agricultural consolidation destabilizing food prices
- Political trust erosion due to money-dominated elections

These are **systemic failures**, not isolated issues.

II. Core Policy Directions

1. Progressive Taxation as Civic Responsibility

- Restore genuinely progressive income taxation
- Implement a graduated **wealth tax on net assets above $10 million**

- Close offshore and financial arbitrage loopholes

Purpose:
To rebalance incentives and repair long-term distortions created since the mid-1980s.

2. Campaign Finance Reform

- End unlimited Super PAC influence
- Full transparency of political donations
- Strengthen public campaign financing

Principle:

Democracy must not be auctioned to the highest bidder.

3. Rebuilding Domestic Capability

- Enact the 25% Made Local framework
- Support local manufacturing ecosystems
- Revitalize small and community-based agriculture
- Enforce antitrust in food, seed, chemical, and distribution markets

4. Social Stability Baseline

Guarantee minimum living standards for:
- Children
- People with disabilities
- The elderly
- The unhoused
- Families in temporary hardship

Rationale:
Societies that allow mass exclusion cannot remain stable.

III. Legislative Evaluation Criteria

Every major economic bill should answer:

1. Does it rebuild real productive capacity?
2. Does it reduce long-term inequality risks?
3. Does it strengthen democratic trust?
4. Does it lower future social and fiscal costs?

Appendix C — Key Data & References

Selected References (APA / Chicago compatible)

Inequality & Taxation
- Piketty, T. (2014). *Capital in the Twenty-First Century*. Harvard University Press.
- Piketty, T. (2020). *Capital and Ideology*. Harvard University Press.
- Stiglitz, J. E. (2012). *The Price of Inequality*. W. W. Norton & Company.

Manufacturing & Deindustrialization
- Autor, D., Dorn, D., & Hanson, G. (2016). *The China Shock. Journal of Economic Perspectives*, 30(3).
- Bureau of Economic Analysis (BEA). *Industry Economic Accounts*.

Agriculture & Food Systems
- U.S. Department of Agriculture (USDA). *Farm Subsidy Distribution Reports*.
- Howard, P. (2016). *Concentration and Power in the Food System*. Bloomsbury.
- Monteiro, C. et al. (2019). *Ultra-Processed Foods and Obesity. Public Health Nutrition*.

Inflation & Structural Constraints
- OECD. (2022). *Global Value Chains and Inflation*.
- Summers, L. (2021). *The Inflation Outlook. Brookings Papers on Economic Activity*.

Climate & Localization
- International Energy Agency (IEA).

Transport and Industry Emissions.
- Jackson, T. (2009). *Prosperity Without Growth*. Earthscan.

Methodological Approach
- Structural economics
- Institutional risk analysis
- Historical comparison
- Long-term civilizational perspective

www.ingramcontent.com/pod-product-compliance
Lightning Source LLC
Chambersburg PA
CBHW062056270326
41931CB00013B/3097